CW01432891

Narcissist

The Ultimate Survival Guide to Protect Yourself from Toxic Relationship, Manipulation, Healing After Emotional/Psychological Abuse and Averting from Narcissistic Personality Disorder

Daniel Peterson

© **Copyright 2019 by ___Daniel Peterson___ - All rights reserved.**

This document is geared towards providing exact and reliable information in regards to the topic and issue covered. The publication is sold with the idea that the publisher is not required to render accounting, officially permitted, or otherwise, qualified services. If advice is necessary, legal or professional, a practiced individual in the profession should be ordered.

- From a Declaration of Principles which was accepted and approved equally by a Committee of the American Bar Association and a Committee of Publishers and Associations.

In no way is it legal to reproduce, duplicate, or transmit any part of this document in either electronic means or in printed format. Recording of this publication is strictly prohibited and any storage of this document is not allowed unless with written permission from the publisher. All rights reserved.

The information provided herein is stated to be truthful and consistent, in that any liability, in terms of inattention or otherwise, by any usage or abuse of any policies, processes, or directions contained within is the solitary and utter responsibility of the recipient reader. Under no circumstances will any legal responsibility or blame be held against the publisher for any reparation, damages, or monetary loss due to the information herein, either directly or indirectly.

Respective authors own all copyrights not held by the publisher.

The information herein is offered for informational purposes solely, and is universal as so. The presentation of the information is without contract or any type of guarantee assurance.

The trademarks that are used are without any consent, and the publication of the trademark is without permission or backing by the trademark owner. All trademarks and brands within this book are for clarifying purposes only and are the owned by the owners themselves, not affiliated with this document.

Table of Contents

Introduction

If you've been living with a narcissist, you probably already had a good idea of what narcissism is. Anyway, let's talk about what a narcissist is, what makes them tick, and why they act the way they do. Once you have a better understanding of these aspects of your partner's personality, you will be better prepared to take and stand up for yourself, and help your partner change into a more loving person.

In general, a narcissist is someone who needs people around to admire them. They feel that they are the most important person in the room, or even in the world, and so they expect everyone to act a certain way toward them because of it. They also have difficulty with empathy and are not able to relate to the fact that others have thoughts, feelings, and ideas independent of them. When this becomes extreme enough, one can be diagnosed with a Narcissistic Personality Disorder, which is generally considered more severe and oftentimes, incurable. But there are ways to deal with narcissism with someone you love, which is the purpose of this book.

Research has shown that there are generally two types of narcissists. The first type has been labeled the **Vulnerable Narcissists**. These people have an outward sense of self-importance, but it is usually hiding some deep vulnerability. They have a weak sense of self and cover this fact up with an inflated sense of importance, and they expect everyone to treat them with devotion and respect in order to feel better about them. Generally, these people are easier to change because, as they are able to develop their self-esteem and feel comfortable as a human being, their need for admiration will naturally disappear.

The second type is called the **Grandiose Narcissist**. This type of narcissist acts more confidently yet less sensitively. People with this type of personality don't have a sense of shame and empathy, and they obviously have a very high self-esteem. They believe in their own greatness which caused them to treat other people quite poorly because they believe no one else can measure up to them. They don't feel the need to treat others with dignity and respect.

Both types of narcissists treat people crudely. Because of their lack of empathy for others, they have no problem hurting or using them for their own gain. The emotions of others have no meaning to them. Moreover, they tend to use manipulation to get whatever they want in the world and tend toward psychopathology, which means that they have difficulty forming relationships like an antisocial person. Remember that they have no ability to relate with others in a meaningful way, so people end up being tools they use to get their own needs met. They don't see others as separate individuals.

Although the causes of narcissism aren't known positively, there are many theories. Most people with narcissism had a difficult parent-child relationship when they were growing up. They might be surrounded by narcissistic people or might have been abused and abandoned as a child and so they developed a self-inflated sense of self in order to cope with life. It's also possible that their parents have ignored them or have been overly critical so they developed a narcissistic behavior. Another causative factor suggests a genetic link. Having a narcissistic family member provides a higher chance of developing a narcissistic personality.

People easily fall for them because, as a tool of manipulation, they are charming. They like to have a good time and they know how to get others to see their eminence in order for them to fall in love. If you have fallen with a narcissist, you know exactly what I'm talking about. Although some of their behaviors can be frustrating at times, but they seem to be able to make their partner happy in many other ways.

That's what makes dealing with a narcissist so tough. There are things you really love about your partner and there are other things that you hate or disgust about their attitude. You may love the excitement your partner provides in your life, how sweet and charming they are at a dinner party, but you may have more difficulty at home when you are alone. Your partner probably treats you very differently than when you are in a public place.

Before deciding whether you want to stay and deal with the techniques in this book to try and improve your relationship, you need to make sure of one thing. Is your relationship abusive? Not all narcissists resort to violence to get their way, but some do exercise physical or emotional abuse toward their partner. If you are being abused, you probably won't be able to do the work necessary for helping yourself and your partner in a safe environment. You might be better off finding a way out rather than trying to change yourself and the person you love. It all depends on how the two of you talk, accept, and deal with the problem.

If you feel like you can make the necessary changes in a safe environment, then you can continue and move forward. The things to note here is that both of you will need to be willing to make changes to help your relationship and to take care of your partner's narcissistic disorder. In a relationship, it takes two to tango, as they say, and it's important to note that your own behavior may be feeding the narcissist. You will need to change how you interact with your partner in order to help that person make changes themselves.

The next chapter will discuss your behavior and how they may be unintentionally encouraging the narcissistic loved one's manner. By changing yourself first, you can make a difference with the attitude of your partner.

Chapter 1: Narcissist and its types

NPD is by no means a one-size-fits-all diagnosis. It is a spectrum. Some narcissists are more harmful and toxic while others are somewhat harmless. Some narcissists are obvious, and others are more subtle. Understanding the differences between these varying kinds of narcissism is key for understanding how each should be handled.

List of all types

Vulnerable Narcissist

Vulnerable or covert narcissists are typically more sensitive than their grandiose counterparts. Vulnerable narcissists are so caught up in fearing rejection or abandonment that they constantly swing between feelings superior to those around them to inferior based upon what is happening at the moment. During times of inferiority, they seek validation from others in order to boost their egos. Oftentimes, these narcissists are hiding their low self-esteem; projecting a persona of the victim. The vulnerable narcissist is always the victim, always demanding sympathy, and always seeking to make those around them see them as perfect. They often appear as quiet and calm, though they also struggle with emotional regulation.

Behind their narcissistic mask lies a person so broken, ashamed, and self-conscious that they put on a front to pretend to the world that they are perfect. These people seem to be overcompensating for their negative feelings and less-than-stellar view of self-worth, often due to trauma suffered in early childhood. Just like the other forms of narcissists, people who develop this form of NPD often do as a coping mechanism to handle any neglect, abuse, or trauma they faced as children. They develop a persona that is perfect, always fixating on doing things exactly right. If they are perfect, they can deny that anything bad that happens is their fault and they can develop an identity encompassed in a victim mentality. They crave the attachment or love they lacked had as children, and fears the abandonment they faced so much that they will do anything to garner the sympathy needed to keep people nearby.

These people care greatly about how those around them perceive them and will go out of their way to build rapport, and even apologize if they think it will get them the desired results. They pride themselves on being seen as outstanding members of their society, but every good deed they do is solely to continue being seen as perfect and receiving the admiration and attention that goes hand in hand with doing good deeds. These are the people who will only do something selfless or generous if there is an audience, or will always, without fail, post their good deeds on social media for people to see. They are more likely to aim for very public careers that leave them engaging with people on the regular, usually in a context where they provide aid to others, as this feeds their need for attention, and also make them appear to be great, upstanding people.

Unlike most of those with personality disorders, vulnerable narcissists are one of the only people who will make threats to harm themselves in order to get attention from those around them, though they will rarely follow through with their threat. These people seek sympathy through any means necessary to get their narcissistic supply, and because of this, they are often emotionally draining. They demand plenty of emotional investment while being quite sensitive as well, making those around them walk on eggshells out of fear of setting off the vulnerable narcissist.

When threatened, the vulnerable narcissist will become quite passive aggressive, as it is never his fault something went wrong. He will passive-aggressively shut out those that threaten him, with comments such as a dejected, "Well, if I am such a big bother, I'll just never go out of my way to talk to you again," fishing for you to either try to convince him that he should stay with you and that you want him there and in his life, or to agree with him, which gives him more material to use to play the victim and garner sympathy from others.

When challenges continue, the vulnerable narcissist is much more explosive than the grandiose narcissist, internalizing the feelings and lashing out. The more vulnerable the narcissist, the more explosive the aggressive will become. As these people already have poor self-esteem, any threat to it is incredibly provocative.

Vulnerable narcissists pride themselves on being a great parent, child, sibling, spouse or whatever else they identify themselves as. For those who live with the narcissist, they likely often hear people say they are so lucky to have the narcissist in their lives, and the person is stuck feeling confused; no one is ever good enough for the narcissist, and the narcissist will be sure to make that clear. Growing up with a narcissistic parent, the child is constantly told he is lucky, but at home, he is constantly criticized. The end result is the child believing that he must be the problem if everyone else thinks his parents are fantastic. This is just the beginning of the damage inflicted by narcissists; the child starts life with a deep-seated belief that there is something inherently wrong with him.

Grandiose Narcissist

Unlike the vulnerable narcissist, the grandiose variety knows that he is better than everyone else and is unafraid of acting as such. These people are much less sensitive than the vulnerable narcissists and do not care as much about what other people think. They are confident, loud, and have high self-esteem, even if it is unwarranted. They are always the hero of every story, and anyone that ever wrongs them is obviously wrong. For the grandiose narcissist, if someone thinks he is less than stellar or disagrees with his stance on something, obviously that person is a plebeian that is too stupid to understand and appreciate genius, and therefore, their opinion means nothing. Anything that critic says will be disregarded as unimportant and untrue.

Likewise, in relationships, the grandiose narcissist does not care if his partner likes him. He does not care about his partner at all, only seeking to use the other person until they are no longer useful. If his partner does not admire and respect him in the way he is so confident he deserves just by virtue of being the perfect, most important, most superior person he knows, he is willing to drop everything and move on to the next victim. He also may have a penchant for indiscreetly carrying multiple affairs, not caring when his primary partner discovers the truth. In fact, he may also accuse his partner of being the one having affairs, or even get angry at his partner when called out.

These narcissists are loud about their achievements, domineering, oftentimes aggressive about getting what they want, and have no qualms about using and hurting people to get what they know they deserve. They brag about every little success that makes them appear better than those they speak to, oftentimes putting down the listener at the same time. The grandiose narcissist will not apologize, even if it will make him look better because he does not care about other people. In his mind, apologizing is something only equals or superiors deserve, and since he is obviously the best person, those he wrongs do not deserve anything.

In contrast with the vulnerable narcissist, who is overcompensating by creating a persona to garner attention and sympathy to validate her self-worth, the grandiose narcissist is not compensating for anything. He is acting on his belief and expectation that he is superior, and he should be treated as such. He may have been told throughout his entire childhood that he is superior to those around him or treated better due to social status or intelligence, and he comes to expect that treatment to carry over into every aspect of his life. He could have been top in his class or the varsity football captain and treated like royalty in school, and he held the expectation that that admiration would follow him for the rest of his life.

The grandiose narcissist thinks that if he believes something, it will become true, regardless of how disordered the thought process is. He will absolutely find some illogical way to justify his beliefs, and he will absolutely believe it. Like children, who will try to wish things into reality, the grandiose narcissist will believe their desires will happen. In their minds, there is absolutely no possible way they are wrong. If you try to provide evidence to support the fact they are wrong, they will brush you off, claiming that what you say is little more than opinion, and deny it has any plausibility. He will also do anything in his power in order to defend his belief and make his desires come true. They will not take no for an answer and will go to extreme lengths to get what they want.

Interestingly, despite grandiose narcissists believing they are much better than everyone else and expecting things to go their way, they are much more flexible when dealing with conflict. Where the vulnerable narcissist erupts into a rage at things not going as expected, the grandiose narcissist makes what he wants to happen. The grandiose narcissist will exploit and manipulate anything necessary in order to get the results he wants; even if that means upholding delusional beliefs that something went exactly according to plan. They are as confident in themselves as they present their own view of reality that they convince some people around them to believe the same.

This may be the ex-husband, who cries to everyone about how much he wanted to be involved in his children's lives, but his monster of an ex-wife poisoned their minds and kept them away from him when in reality, he abandoned his children and has been avoiding their calls and attempts at contact. Despite the fact that he abandoned them, he believes wholeheartedly that his spouse alienated his children from him and shifts all of the blame to her. After all, he has always been a fantastic father and his children adored him. Those around him will take his words at face value, unaware that he simply no longer found his children useful now that they were old enough to question him, and he himself will believe the delusions he has declared. These narcissists are so convincing in their manipulation that they even manage to manipulate themselves into believing their delusions.

Malignant Narcissist

While some narcissists are little more than annoying and exhausting to interact with, a small percentage are downright toxic. These are known as malignant narcissists, and they are utterly vicious, destructive, and inhumane. These people teeter somewhere between both NPD and ASPD, often embodying all of the identifying traits of narcissists with some of ASPDs antisocial behavior tendencies, along with sadistic tendencies and, oftentimes, paranoia. These narcissists thrive off of inflicting pain and torment wherever they go.

Described by some as the epitome of evil, these people are the quintessential villain who wants nothing more than to watch the world burn. These people, though they present as grandiose and charming, have a fragile ego and are sensitive to any sort of criticism. They feel an intense desire for recognition, and they envy those around them that have the success they desire. They work hard to achieve success and present themselves as successful, though this is solely to get the admiration they desire. In reality, however, deep within themselves, they feel crushing self-doubt, inferiority, and emptiness, and they feel paranoid that their true selves will be discovered, or even worse, that others are actively seeking to expose them.

These narcissists are outwardly charming and sometimes promiscuous or seductive, but despite this gravitation toward physical intimacy with others, they are unable to develop any truly meaningful relationship. Any relationship pursued is for their own self-interest, and when they have satisfied whatever desire they had, they suddenly shift to cold and apathetic toward whoever was being used.

As seen in antisocial personality disorder, the malignant narcissist vehemently dislikes social conventions, and as such, tends to lie and steal. They have a blatant disregard for the law, and may even commit violent crimes or form terrorist organizations. These antisocial tendencies lend themselves to acts of violence or sadism, which is little more than a way of self-affirmation. By hurting and destroying those around him, the malignant narcissist feels gratification. They lack any and all forms of empathy for others, unlike other narcissists, who may feel some reduced capacity of empathy, but are still capable of feeling regret or remorse.

While manipulation is a key feature of all narcissists, those with malignant narcissism are actively seeking to manipulate others, intentionally honing their skills and calculating every move to get exactly what they want. The malignant narcissists are much more forceful in their attempts to manipulate, even if their forcefulness comes with a cost of decreasing how subtle the attempts are. Unlike how many other narcissists' opportunistic manipulation, the malignant narcissist proactively manipulates others, enjoying the process almost as much as enjoying the suffering the victim feels.

Like all narcissists, the malignant narcissists crave attention; this is a vital form of emotional and mental nourishment for them. Unlike other narcissists, however, malignant narcissists have no preference between positive or negative attention. They do not care what other people think about them, so long as other people are actively thinking about them. A negative thought about them is still good enough, and sometimes, these people will intentionally play the villain in order to garner negative attention intentionally.

The malignant narcissist is the most toxic form of narcissism there is, and these people should be avoided if at all possible. They love to cause suffering, reveling in the pain of others. They intentionally inflict harm with no regard for suffering or social conventions and do what they want when they want. These narcissists are dangerous and do not have the mental capacity to keep them from hurting, or even killing, their targets if they desire to do so.

Chapter 2: Traits of a Narcissist

The definition of a psychopath is a person who suffers from a mental disorder who could manifest violent or abnormal social behavior. They are mainly considered aggressive and unstable, which allows them to cause major mental, emotional, and sometimes even physical abuse on people around them.

If you haven't seen the dark side of your narcissist, it might shock you to learn that the narcissist is a psychopath. They have deep-seated mental issues that likely reach back as far as their childhood. This is why it is pretty much impossible for a person with NPD to recover.

Many in-depth studies of narcissistic and psychopathic behavior have found certain behavioral patterns that they follow. These are tendencies that you are likely going to notices in nearly all narcissists, and many have very similar personalities.

Even though everybody displays narcissistic tendencies from varying degrees, they are not to the point of being labeled a psychopath. Only if these behaviors start to cause abnormalities in social functioning is the person then seen to be a full blown narcissist.

Manipulation

Narcissists have a plethora of manipulation techniques that they can use at any moment. It would take a while to go through every single one, but it is helpful to know them so that you better understand their true self, so we will touch on the more common ones. Once you know those, it's easy to spot the rest. In fact, we've touched on one already, gas lighting.

The first one, and likely the most used, is shaming. This can be in private or in public. The purpose of the shame is often two-fold, and can use a combination of their other techniques. This is something you will likely start to notice is that their tactics will overlap, and the goal of most is to manipulate you to do what they want you to. The two-fold purpose of shaming is, one, to up their own intelligence and worth, and two, to make you feel less than them.

This shaming is used to encourage you to submit to your abuser. This shaming will like thoughts like, "They seem to know more than me, so it might be best for me to take my cues from them and then, maybe, I can deserve their praise," may cross their mind. With this mentality, everything you say and do will be geared towards making sure your abuser is happy and approves, which is exactly what they wanted to achieve.

Another manipulation tactic is playing the role of the victim. This normally starts when the abused is in a spot where they feel inconvenienced by the demands of the narcissist. Here's an example:

Amanda is a little low on cash after her job laid her off since her company had to make budget cuts. She is going into her third month without a job, and she has to turn to friends and family for financial support. She has been asking Brian for some help over the past few weeks, and at first, he was happy to help her out. But now her financial needs are making a noticeable dent in his own finances.

For the umpteenth time, Amanda has asked Brian for some cash, but Brain isn't as willing this time. "If I give you the money I have on hand, I won't be able to cover my bills. I can't help out this time. I hope you understand."

"I can't believe you could treat me this way. I literally have no job and I have to have money in order to survive. But of course, getting "behind" on your own bills is much worse than my problems. Sorry for bothering you."

Brian still gives her the money and says that he will use his next paycheck to catch up on his bills. Was Amanda right to demand what she did from her friend?

First off, Brian is in control of his own finances, so he has the right to choose how he uses his money that he works hard for. Choosing to help Amanda or not is up to him and nobody else should hold his decision against him.

Second, it's important to remember that Amanda has been without a job for three months, which is likely more than enough time to get another job to help her meet her financial needs. The fact that she is choosing to rely on others to help meet her financial needs shows that she is likely enjoying the setup of surviving without having to work for it.

She still manages to manipulate Brian into putting her interests in front of his own by making him feel guilty. She is playing the role of the victim. She highlights her problems and minimizes Brian's to make him come off as greedy and unreasonable.

The next manipulation tactic is conditional love. This manipulation tactic provides the abused with enough affection to make them want to be on their abuser's good side. Narcissists will often use this when the victim makes them happy or does something that makes them look good. It works as positive reinforcement so that the victim wants to continue doing the good work.

Genuine love is supposed to be unconditional. It shouldn't come with strings attached. Real love loves the person despite their shortcomings. Unfortunately, a narcissist is unable to do this.

If their victim does anything that they don't approve of, they will without their affection and love, and will make their victim feel undeserving of their love. It's only after they apology and acknowledge their mistakes that the narcissist will "forgive" them.

The last manipulation tactic we'll talk about is blaming you for everything. They use this to make sure that their image stays clean while making their victim feel accountable for everything. Narcissists never want to appear wrong in any situation, and so they will do whatever it takes to make sure that they never get blamed for anything bad.

They will look for a scapegoat, which will typically be their current victim, and they will turn around the situation to make that person feel bad. This will cause their victim to feel unworthy, which causes them to hold tighter to their abuser out of fear of being alone.

Most of them time, narcissists will also make sure to let others know of the victim's shortcomings. This overly done, with the victim completely aware that other people in their world are aware of the ways they have messed up. This causes the victim to feel embarrassed, and it makes them submit to their abuser to show remorse and a want to correct their mistakes.

All of these different strategies for manipulation don't only make the victim act in a certain fashion in that moment, but it also instills a long-term want to keep the relationship healthy for the foreseeable future. This destroys the victim's free-will and self-worth so that they are reliant on the abuser. This gives the narcissist the ability to control their actions.

What does the narcissist get out of all of this control? Narcissists thrive on praise and admiration. Having people under their spell gives them the ability to get a hit whenever they need it. Their victim's endless need to please them gives then a consistent source of admiration.

On top of this, they also feel like they are entitled to all of this and can use people however they need to. In their mind, they are better than everybody so they have the right to make others feel bad and make the subordinate. By controlling your life, they are helping you out since they think they know better than you do.

The need for attention

Narcissists not only want constant attention but will also demand the same. That behavior can be something as simple as constantly following you around the house, saying outrageous things to grab your attention, or asking you to do things for them. Narcissists' wants for validation is as constant as their need for attention. They require constant validation, and it doesn't count unless it comes from others. Even then, it doesn't mean much.

A narcissist's need for attention and validation is like a black hole that can never be filled. You can channel all your positivity, support, and attention, but even then, it will not fulfill the narcissist's need. Regardless of how much and how often you tell a narcissist about your love and admiration for them, it will never be enough. A narcissist's psyche is such that he truly believes that he is incapable of being loved by others. In spite of the façade of self-absorption and a sense of grandiose, a narcissist is often insecure and afraid of never being able to measure up. He craves praise and approval from others because it helps to bolster his fragile ego.

Extremely controlling

Narcissists are almost always disappointed with the way life turns out, so they try to do everything they can to control and shape it according to their wishes. They not only need to be controlled, but they demand that they must be in control. Their sense of entitlement and superiority only fuels their belief that they must be in control of everything. Not just that, narcissists will also have a specific storyline in their mind for every character in their life. They expect others to behave and react in the manner they have imagined in their mind. When this doesn't happen—in fact, it seldom does—it just makes narcissists feel unsettled and upset. They are incapable of predicting what will happen next since you are going "off-script." So, don't be surprised if you notice that narcissists will often demand that you must speak and behave in a specific manner so that they can retain their sense of control. You are merely a character in the play that the narcissists are directing. Narcissists fail to see that others are separate entities with their own thoughts and desires.

The unmistakable feeling of superiority

Narcissists tend to live in a two-dimensional world where everything is either black or white. Everyone and everything can be classified as good or bad, right or wrong, and superior or inferior. There exists a specific hierarchy in their minds, and they are obviously present in the top tier. A narcissist will feel safe only when he thinks he is at the top. A narcissist always feels like he must be the absolute best; he must always be right and should be able to control everyone around him. A narcissist also thinks people must always do things the narcissist's way.

It is quite interesting to note that a narcissist can also experience this feeling of superiority by being the absolute worst, or even the most upset. If they feel like this, they tend to think that they are entitled to receive concern or empathy, and they may even think that they have the right to hurt others or demand an apology to make things right. A sense of absolute superiority and entitlement are amongst the defining traits of a narcissist.

Absence of boundaries

Narcissists are incapable of seeing where they end and where you begin. They are quite similar to toddlers. They seem to think that everything belongs to them, that everyone thinks as they do, and that everyone wants the same things they do. In fact, narcissists will be quite shocked and affronted if they realize this isn't true. If narcissists desire something from you, they will go to great lengths to get what they want. The narcissists can be extremely persistent in their quest for getting what they want from you or others.

Shrugs all responsibility

A narcissist does love to be in control, but he will never want to accept any responsibility for the turn of events unless everything goes the way he planned and the desired results are obtained. When things don't proceed according to his plan or when he receives any criticism, the narcissist will conveniently shift all the responsibility and the blame onto others. It has to be someone else's fault because narcissists are the epitome of perfection, at least, according to themselves. Since they are perfect, if things don't go as planned, it must be someone else's fault. At times, the blame can be quite generalized—the police, the management, the teachers, the government, and so on. At times, the blame can be quite specific. The narcissist might pick a specific individual to blame like his parents, the law, or even the judge. Usually, a narcissist tends to blame the person that he is quite close to.

To enable the fragile façade of perfection, a narcissist will often find someone to blame. If you happen to be the person the narcissist is closest to, then be prepared to take the blame. You will be the safest person to blame because the chances of you leaving the narcissist are quite slim, and this makes him feel safe.

Desire for perfection

Narcissists have a desire for perfection and expect it from everyone and everything around them as well as themselves. They believe that they must be perfect, you must be perfect, and the events in life must be as expected and that their life needs to unfold precisely in the manner they envisioned.

This exaggerated need for demanding the impossible is the reason why a narcissist often feels quite miserable and dissatisfied. Their constant need for perfection makes them complain constantly.

Complete lack of empathy

Only when you can understand others and can see where they are coming from will you be able to empathize with them. A narcissist cannot empathize with others. In fact, it is safe to say that narcissists are devoid of all empathy. They are selfish, self-absorbed, and self-centered. These traits prevent a narcissist from ever being able to understand the feelings of others fully. Narcissists seldom give a conscious thought about what others might think or feel; after all, they expect others to think as they do. Also, a narcissist might not experience guilt or remorse and may rarely—if ever—apologize.

That said, narcissists are quite adept at identifying any alleged threats, anger, and rejection from others around him. At the same time, they are quite oblivious to the feelings and emotions of others around them. They often misinterpret simple minute facial expressions and are biased while interpreting the same. Unless you display your emotions dramatically, narcissists are incapable of accurately assuming what you are experiencing. Even saying something as simple as "I love you" or "I am sorry" can backfire easily if the narcissists are in a foul mood. They might not believe you and will assume that your comment was an attack instead.

Apart from this, if your words and expressions are not in sync, the narcissists will respond incorrectly. It is the reason why most narcissists fail to understand sarcasm or jokes and think of them as a personal attack. Their inability to properly read body language is another reason why narcissists aren't empathetic. They cannot perceive emotions correctly, and they tend to misinterpret them. They also don't believe that you can think and act in a manner different from theirs.

Narcissists cannot understand the nature of feelings. They don't understand how feelings manifest. They believe their feelings are often the result of an external force or action. They don't realize that their feelings are a manifestation of their biochemistry, their thoughts, and their perceptions. Simply put, narcissists believe you are responsible for what they feel, especially all the negative ones.

They come to this conclusion because you deviated from their plan or because you made them feel insecure. So, the only logical recourse in a narcissist's mind is to blame you. This apparent lack of empathy certainly makes it quite difficult to establish a true and meaningful relationship with a narcissist.

Chapter 3: Narcissist Personality Disorder and Treatment Options

What Causes NPD?

In the modern society, the number of people with narcissistic behaviors has increased tremendously. It would be right to state that most of the domestic violence cases are tied to narcissist relationships. The issue is most people do not realize that their partner is a narcissist and assume that the violence they face is part of the normal family. There are relationships that have unending issues that usually result in violence or rather a physical fight. For a normal family, it is easy to solve conflicts through mutual respect and cohesiveness. However, in the case where conflicts are unending and it appears that one of the partners takes pleasure in it, then it is not a normal or healthy relationship. As such, it would be helpful if people learned about narcissists and how they manifest various behavioral aspects in a relationship.

Narcissists have different cognitive aspects compared to other people. These are people who are preoccupied with fantasies such as ideal love, beauty, brilliance, power, and unlimited success. They lack a sense of reality in each of these things. The believe they are entitled to each of the noted aspects and they do not care about the people they hurt along the way. They are incapable of comprehending the negative emotions that they cause people. As such, they believe they are unique and special which makes them think that they should be treated in a preferential manner. These are unreasonable entitlements and expectations of proper treatment and automatic compliance with their expectations. Due to this, they will subject their partners to difficult situations without caring for the harm they are causing. For instance, they may ask you to quit your job, they may force you not to accept a promotion and expect you to adhere to it. They dislike things that are likely to improve their partner's position or those that are likely to give them freedom. Most people who have been with a narcissist will tell you that they had to give up their dreams with the intention of making their partner happy.

Additionally, these are interpersonally exploitative individuals. All their actions are calculated, they need to feed on their victim's emotions. They enjoy creating confusion in their victim's life. There is nothing that gives them more pleasure than to see their victims suffering for their benefit. For instance, they bring in another person in a relationship without regard for their partner's feelings. Normally if a person starts seeing another person, or if they start getting back with their ex-lovers, they will hide this truth. For a narcissist they will do things intentionally so that you can know, they want to create jealousy in you so that you start competing for them. They will stay and watch how you are struggling to please them. Also, they do as much as they can to make it appear that it is your fault that the relationship is having problems. It is right to state this as inhumane, and because most people do not realize this, they are drawn into competition with the intention to prove themselves.

Generally, a narcissist is an arrogant individual. A person who does something and manipulates you and those close to you and has a high level of arrogance. When you are in a relationship, he/she goes about telling family and friends that you have emotional instability. A narcissist is truly someone to avoid. They are boastful and pretentious especially when they are relating to other people. Truly you can be confused by a person who treats you poorly but treats other people with respect. Thoughts about being the one with the problem and responsible for the instability in the relationship will automatically come into your mind. If you are in such a position in your life, the person you are with is a narcissist. The reason for this is because they want approval and need excessive admiration from other people. They will make you the 'bad' person in the relationship so that they can achieve what they need.

Being in love with a narcissist is more like being in a prison. They use different tricks and strategies to manipulate you. They are the ones who spotted the qualities that make us human such as compassion, love, and sentimentality and used them against you.

It is disturbing and one will have numerous questions as to what they did wrong or what they failed to do that made this person disappear. But as we will discover, this is what they intended from the beginning; they cannot settle for a romantic relationship from its beginning to the end.

In a healthy relationship partners are focused on building each other they find a way for both of them to work. In this relationship, people tend to talk and listen to each other to find a solution to the problem they are having. To a narcissist they always take the lead they want to dominate the conversation and make things about themselves.

Their sense of importance makes them think that as their partner you are there to serve them and whatever they do to you and for you is in line with finding their satisfaction. Thus, as the victim, it is difficult to express your feelings, needs, and rights. In another relationship, you will tell someone you are sad because they offended you in this manner. When you are with a narcissist you will learn that there is neither need nor room for you to express your feelings. They are quick to dismiss them and imply that there is no reason to feel that way and you are the reason why you feel that way.

Therefore, it is important that you watch for the noted things and falling for fantasy. Narcissists could be charming and magnetic; they are experts in creating a flattering and fantastical self-image that will lure you. What you get attached to is their lofty dreams and confidence as they tease your self-esteem and employ a seductive approach that will leave you regretting meeting them. It is easy to be caught in their spider web thinking that they will always be there to satisfy your longing to feel loved, more alive and more important. This is just a fantasy that in the end, you will pay dearly.

The Diagnostic Criteria For NPD

The DSM-5 states that in order to be diagnosed with NPD, one must exhibit at least 5 of the following 9 traits, with the traits beginning to present persistently by early adulthood, in a wide variety of different contexts and situations.

Grandiose sense of self-importance

The narcissist believes he is the most important person there is in whatever context he is in. At work, he must have the key job, and he will go through the mental gymnastics, no matter how delusional they sound to the rest of us, to convince himself that his job as a janitor is the only reason the entire building is running, or that the CNA is the only reason the patient who just underwent major heart surgery is still alive. While janitors and CNAs are undeniably necessary for their industries to keeping their businesses running, they are by no means the most important, the most difficult to replace, or crucial positions. In a relationship, she is the best thing that ever has and will ever happen to her partner. Without her, her partner would be completely helpless and miserable, or in some cases, even dead.

An obsession with fantasies of unlimited or unrealistic successes, influence, power, looks, or love

As the narcissist is the best person in the world, he deserves nothing but the best in his mind, to the point where he obsesses and fantasizes over absolute perfection at all times, regardless of how unrealistic his standards may be. He will never be satisfied unless he achieves or receives absolute perfection in every aspect of his life, which of course, means that he will never be satisfied as his standards are impossible.

Delusional sense of uniqueness

The narcissist believes she is absolutely unique or special, and therefore, she must only associate with other special people who are worthy of her attention. The narcissist will only seek out other people or institutions that are high-class enough for her, even if she herself may not belong where she believes. Likewise, those not worthy of her attention or those unaware of her perceived specialness may find themselves a victim of her scorn should they make the mistake of approaching her without her express permission. These are the people treating waiters as less than human because their sole purpose on life must clearly be to serve the customers.

A need for continuous and excessive admiration

One of the defining keys of NPD, the narcissist has an innate need to validate his or her delusions through constant and excessive attention and admiration. They seek those they know will provide this, whether it is a friend, relative, coworker, or romantic interest, preferring those whose personalities lend them to being empathetic because the empathetic are the ones most likely to provide the narcissist with the supply of praise, admiration, and love the narcissist craves.

A distorted sense of entitlement

Along with the belief that she is the most special person in the world, the narcissist expects to be treated as such. She believes that everything she desires will simply happen due to her being deserving of such. She believes she deserves the praise and success she wants without having to earn it. While there is a normal sense of entitlement, in which people justify their self-esteem or expectations of success on past accomplishments, the narcissist has no such justification for her expectation.

Manipulative

Particularly in cases with toxic narcissists, those with NPD often manipulate those around them. They put up a front, hiding their true selves behind a mask and convincing everyone around them that their persona is who they really are. They are often charismatic, able to convince everyone around them, and only those closest to the narcissist find themselves victim to brainwashing, gas lighting, and countless lies that may only become obvious if the narcissist lets his mask slip. The narcissist is never wrong and will use every tactic in his playbook necessary to convince you and the rest of the world that he is not the problem.

Lacking empathy

Empathy is defined as the ability to cognitively and emotionally experience and understand the emotions or thoughts of someone else while concurrently being aware of his or her own thoughts or emotions. This is what allows us to understand what those around us are feeling, which aids in our survival as a social species. When we understand and care for those around us, we are more likely to engage in socially constructive behavior, meaning we are all more likely to survive. Narcissists lack this empathy, making it difficult or impossible for them to understand what those around them feel. With no regard for others' thoughts or feelings, the narcissist has no qualms about manipulating or hurting those around him; for her own benefit or to confirm her delusions of grandeur.

Envying others, or believing that others envy him or her

As narcissists often believe they deserve success without any effort, they envy when those around them have what they want and have yet to achieve. He may be unable to compliment or congratulate a friend or loved one when they have succeeded, instead of detracting from the success by minimizing what was done or shifting attention back to the narcissist. For example, if his friend just bought a house, the narcissist may shrug it off and say most people buy houses, and that 15% down payment was nothing; it would have been impressive had he paid cold hard cash for the house instead of getting a mortgage. Besides, the bank currently owns the house until it is paid off, so is buying really any different than renting with extra responsibilities in the short term? At least the narcissist is renting, so when the roof needs to be replaced or the plumbing fails, the narcissist doesn't have to pay for it. The narcissist may then go on to tell himself that the friend secretly envies him because renting is so much less stressful than owning. In his mind, he tries to shift his own envy around into the other person envying him instead.

Haughty and arrogant behavioral patterns or attitudes

The narcissist may come across as haughty and arrogant, or otherwise aggressive when discussing those she believes are less important than her. Watch interactions with waiters, cashiers, or others in service fields: The narcissist will jump on the opportunity to ream a waiter for dropping something. Not only will she behave in condescending, abrasive ways, but she may also take an offensive stance, such as standing upright, quick, sharp movements, or hands on the hips. The narcissist will often enjoy this process as well; it feeds into her delusion that she is superior to the other person; pair this with the lack of empathy and the attack can be ruthless and unending.

Chapter 4: The Actions and Thoughts of a Narcissist

A narcissist has been described above as a person who buries their true self and expresses themselves with a false self; a persona that often clashes with other people because the narcissist is highly conceited. The major attribute of a narcissist is extreme love of them self which they use to avoid being seen or always feeling wounded. Deep down the narcissists feel worthless and they painfully cannot admit this. Especially not in front of others.

Typical Behaviors

The following is a checklist of the behavior of a narcissist towards their partner.

Love-bombing

This is one of the most popular behaviors a narcissist employs when they realize that a person seeking love has let their guard down. Love bombing can be described as the deliberate attempts of influencing an individual by greatly endearing them. And true to the narcissists' sentiments, love bombing feels well, because it makes one create this perfect picture in their mind. Narcissists idealize their partner to get them to reciprocate these feelings and idealize them as well. Ranging from love notes in every place you visit daily, highly flattering comments, surprise appearances, and frequent messaging, the narcissists use these to manipulate one into spending more time with them and not with other people. They try to create an impression of themselves to you that they are the perfect partner, capture your attention and affection, and then shape up your role in the relationship as the support system.

Most people struggle with admitting that a person can be a narcissist if they say they adore them. However, they fail to differentiate between love and affection that grows gradually from the immediate love-bombing that a narcissist shows them. Simply put, love-bombing from a narcissist is affection and adoration that is just too good to be true.

Gas-lighting

Gas-lighting identifies as a consistent mode of encoding and it is among a narcissist's favorite tools. It refers to how a narcissist brainwashes their partner and gradually makes them lose a good sense of themselves. They are calculative and they know just how much a statement that they tell their partner will appropriately marginalize them and cause them to question their identity. To keep up with their gas lighting tool, narcissists are always lying, exaggerating things, become aggressive when criticized and hardly admit their flaws, and they always tend to cross boundaries. Exaggerations are used to elevate themselves while downgrading their partner and lies are meant to distort facts and leave the partner with questions at all times. They always intimidate their partner whenever they are accused of something and can even resort to fighting when their negative behavior is pointed out.

Discarding People They No Longer Want

In one way or another, a narcissist is bound to discard you. The one thing that you should know is that a narcissist is okay with or without you. Your feelings and values mean nothing to them. You can tell this by the way they lack remorse for their wrongful doings, and how they lack empathy and understanding.

In the love-bombing phase, you might be made to believe that you mean everything to the narcissist, not realizing that you are just an object of satisfaction and not a necessary partner whose package is a human being with a heart and soul. Whether it is the narcissist who ends the relationship, or you are the one who leaves or however the relationship blows up, there is always the next target waiting and being groomed to replace the object.

Further, a narcissist's mode of discarding is always brutal since they will accuse you of outrageous things, and even characterize you as if you are the narcissist yourself. They will discredit you to anyone who tries to listen to your story. The worst part about the narcissist's desertion is that it tears our souls and humanity up and disorients our safe and valued place. Yet the narcissist has to use this tool to preserve their false selves by rejecting your real self.

Feeling Superior and Entitled

Whenever a narcissist is interacting with other people, even in a relationship, there is always a hierarchy, with themselves at the top of the ladder. At the top is their safe place and they cannot allow anyone to be above them. They have the dire need to be the most competent, owning everything and having everything done their way. At times they even feel misused or injured and demand concern and apologies from you even if you truly did not hurt them.

They always want to get all of their partner's attention, always following you and talking to you to capture your attention. They need your validation and they want to get only positive words from you. Yet no matter how much you show them love, they do not believe that anyone can indeed love them. Hence to keep up their fragile egos, they always want more because they do not believe that what you give them is enough.

Perfectionist Behavior

We tend to throw around the word "perfect" like it is some sort of an easy thing to attain. When placed under such expectations, it is easy for some people to reason out and say that perfectionism is logically not attainable. The worst happens when the voice of a narcissist takes away their logic and makes them believe in perfectionism. A narcissist has strange perfectionist expectations of the people around them, most especially their partners. Due to their false perfect image, they tend to expect that events should occur exactly as they deem fit, and that life would play out in alignment with their beliefs. Due to this, the narcissist is always dissatisfied with what you do and is always complaining.

Failure to Claim Responsibility but Deflecting to Others

Unless something goes exactly how they wanted it to, narcissists do not claim the responsibility of their mistakes. They do not like to feel imperfect or give others a window to criticize them. They have to blame someone to not appear like they made a mistake. Sometimes the blame is generalized, for instance blaming their boss, but most often, the blame will fall on their partner. They find their partner to be the best blaming target because the partner will most likely pardon them or leave them. Indeed, it is so obvious that someone who envisions themselves as perfect and superior cannot accept responsibility for their mistakes.

Lack of Empathy

Extreme arrogance and self-absorption rarely go hand in hand with empathy, and that is a behavior found in narcissists. Despite having the ability to detect how other people feel, narcissists fail to show compassion. They are interested in fulfilling their needs with little or no regard at all for their partner. They mightily struggle with being empathetic since their minds are full of how they can get you hooked into their needs and this inhibits their ability to be objective about how other people feel.

Emotional Reasoning

This identifies as some type of cognitive distortion through which a narcissist convinces themselves of something being true without facts and even while others convince them otherwise. They tend to interpret their emotional reasoning as the reality and the first problem that this causes is that it makes them believe that they are not worth deep within them. It makes them never appreciate any form of love from their partner because they have convinced themselves that they are not lovable. They even overlook any form of solid evidence and instead rely on their assumed truth.

The basic assumption that overlooks facts is "There must be a reason for how I am feeling right now." Due to this character, it is hard to reason together with a narcissist and makes them see and believe your side of view.

Cannot Connect Emotionally

Narcissists lack the capacity to connect with other people emotionally since they have a constant need for self-protection. They cannot align their feelings with those of any other person and they cannot view things from others' perspective. They want people to respond to their pain and not feel the pain of others. Yet it is impossible to effectively get intimate with a person who cannot compromise some of their standards or even trust you. Essentially, vulnerability requires trust, and this is something that narcissists are unable to develop with their partner. This explains why they engage in a one-sided relationship since they cannot see eye to eye with their partner. Even if they may be with you physically and showering you with love, in the real sense narcissists are not with you.

Cannot Work in a Team

Now, any collaborative work needs a good understanding of another person's true feelings. It requires a consideration of how the action you take might affect the other person and if any decision you make will make both of you happy. This is the kind of attitude that makes romantic relationships thrive because you strive to not do things that will have highly negative impacts on the person you love. However, a narcissist does not understand or try to give provisions for their partner's feelings. This way, they are unable to be a team player. Most importantly, their aim is to control their partner and not be on the same level as them.

Chapter 5: Can Treatment be Successful?

Narcissism is particularly tricky to treat and manage; as the individual with NPD inherently believes he is perfect as he is, he is not particularly open to the idea of seeking any help to fix some flaw he does not believe exists. The pervasive denial and stubbornness make treating NPD incredibly difficult, as you cannot use therapeutic techniques on an unwilling patient, and only someone legitimately seeking to better him will actually benefit from therapy. Because of this, NPD is largely regarded to be untreatable, especially when severe. However, for the few who are open to admitting they have a problem, psychotherapy is the most frequent treatment for narcissism. There are two types of psychotherapy that have been found effective in treating narcissism: Cognitive behavioral therapy (CBT) and psychodynamic therapy.

Cognitive behavioral therapy

This therapy focuses on restructuring distorted, unrealistic thoughts in order to alter feelings and ultimately, alter the behavior as a result. CBT recognizes the feedback loop in thoughts influencing feelings, which influence behavior, which influences thoughts, and so on indefinitely. This form of therapy interrupts the feedback loop by questioning and challenging thoughts that are unhelpful, incorrect, or unrealistic, using a variety of techniques. It is a short-term therapy with long-term results and is often quite successful when the patient is cooperative. It typically averages between 5 and 20 sessions, focusing solely on teaching the patient coping mechanisms and tools to repair disordered thoughts rather than aiming to fix any sort of past trauma that may have caused the NPD in the first place. That does not mean the therapist is uninterested in exploring any traumas; rather, the belief is that just as the reason an arm is broken is irrelevant to a doctor's treatment of the problem, the therapist is interested in fixing the current problems caused by the behavior rather than focusing on the past.

Through multiple sessions with a therapist, the narcissist gradually learns how to identify and replace grandiose or distorted thoughts with more accurate, productive thinking. This is done through journaling, homework assignments, and practice with the therapist and in real life situations. The narcissist will learn how to identify problematic behaviors and thinking and begin to deconstruct it, choosing more productive behaviors instead. As they begin implementing more productive behaviors, their thought processes should begin to improve as well, with an end goal of beginning to fix the broken self-esteem and self-worth the narcissist carries.

As a narcissist has built up an entire persona based on distorted beliefs that CBT will aim to deconstruct, tearing them down can be painstaking, but ultimately can be effective if the narcissist is truly open to receiving the treatment. Along with cognitive restructuring, the narcissist's

CBT sessions will likely include behavior modification, which is learning to cease unproductive or harmful behaviors with healthier, productive actions. For narcissists with deep-rooted fears of rejection or failure, they may also be treated with exposure therapy, during which they will gradually be exposed to their most feared scenarios, so they eventually become less afraid of them.

Psychodynamic therapy

Like CBT, psychodynamic therapy is a form of psychotherapy. It is a talk therapy based on psychoanalysis with an emphasis on the patient's interactions and relationship with the world around him or her. During this therapy, patients are encouraged to discuss anything on their minds and how they feel about the thoughts they have. As the patient discusses his thoughts and feelings, the therapist asks clarifying and guiding questions that allow for the identification of patterns of thinking the patient exhibits. The ultimate goal of identifying these patterns is to lessen or eliminate symptoms of NPD by increasing self-awareness, self-esteem, which many vulnerable narcissists lack, and an understanding of why the narcissist follows the patterns in the first place. By bringing the reasons to light, the patient is able to resolve the conflicts and therefore eliminate the need to behave narcissistically.

This therapy works by developing a thorough understanding of negative or repressed feelings in order to improve current experiences and relationships. The patient learns to identify how something that happened in the past is directly impacting current behavior, and by understanding that correlation, the patient is able to begin correcting it. It seeks to bring acccptance of the past, teaching the patient to identify who he or she truly is and use that information as a way to reconfigure one's self.

Think of the person as a puzzle; the narcissist's puzzle is put together incorrectly, with pieces forced together. It kind of resembles the general colors of what the image it is supposed to present, but does not paint a clear picture. Psychodynamic therapy teaches the narcissist to disassemble the puzzle and rebuild it the way it was supposed to be. The goal here is to create a more functional identity that does not require the crutches of narcissistic tendencies in order to validate or protect itself.

Family or marital therapy

While it may be tempting to take a narcissist to therapy in order to get treatment, beware the triangulation that can occur between the therapist and yourself. The narcissist may have the charisma to charm the therapist onto her side, and if she does, you will have two people telling you that you are at the heart of all of your perceived problems. If the narcissist somehow fails to convince the therapist, then she will learn from the therapist in order to be less obvious and more convincing in the future. Just as it is typically not recommended to take your abuser to therapy with you, it is often not recommended to take a narcissist to joint therapy either. Consider this as an option after extensive individual therapy.

Chapter 6: Other Personality Disorders Related to Narcissism

As narcissistic tendencies appear to becoming more generally accepted it may be increasingly difficult to decide if someone you know has NPD or not. Its increasing acceptance is, in part, related to the perceived need for narcissism in leaders. This need has led to an increase in leaders with narcissistic tendencies and every new political or business leader seems to have more than the one before! Whilst it can be a valuable asset in leadership it can also be a destructive force.

If someone you know and care about displays the following symptoms it is likely that they have NPD and you should convince them to get medical help at the earliest possibility.

The following symptoms have already been discussed in this book:

1. Sense of self importance

2. Living in a fantasy world where they are powerful, rich, and beautiful and have the perfect life.

3. A belief that they are special and only over special people can truly understand them.

4. Needs constant attention and admiration from others.

5. They feel they are entitled to the best of everything; they are, after all, superior to everyone else!

6. A lack of empathy for other people; their feelings and personal anguish

7. A strong belief that others are envious of them, although they are actually envious of others.

8. They tend to be arrogant and self-absorbed; oblivious of their effect on others.

9. They react quickly and usually very badly to any criticism. In fact, people with NPD are usually very good at criticizing others but they do not like to receive this criticism returned to them.

However; there are extra indicators that can suggest to you that the person you know is suffering from NPD:

1. Low Self Esteem

This may seem surprising but people with NPD are often over the top to cover their own self esteem issues. In fact, it is this low self-esteem which is often the main driving force behind their lives. They spend the majority of their time striving to prove themselves; they want to believe in themselves and others to believe in them but they never feel their accomplishments are enough.

The result is driving them onwards to achieve bigger and better things; at all costs.

Of course, people with NPD tend to be expert at portraying a high level of self-esteem and bravado. Perhaps the biggest clue to this issue is that they are constantly seeking compliments from others; if they are not forthcoming they will compliment themselves by bragging and boasting!

2. Self Righteous and Defensive

The bigger their ego appears to be the more important it becomes to defend it from other people attacking. This means the trigger for their defense mechanism becomes shorter and shorter; resulting in even the slightest criticism or comment triggering it. At this point they will be certain they are right and that there path is the only one that can be chosen; they will also become exceptionally stubborn as they defend their actions; regardless of logic.

They must cling to the knowledge that they are right to avoid destroying their fragile ego and exposing their low self-esteem.

3. Quick to Anger

If those who are criticizing someone with an NPD do not back down or change their mind, then the person with the narcissistic personality disorder is likely to react with anger. This is the last, explosive defense mechanism of someone who feels their fears and insecurities are about to be exposed. Worse than this they are likely to be about to re-feeling their emotions and humiliation from the past and transferring this anger to the present day; thereby exploding and taking the current situation out of proportion. The response is likely to baffle the person who had been criticizing them and possibly even frighten them; it will probably end the discussion.

4. Projecting Traits

Someone with NPD sees themselves as right and perfect; others are beneath them. Should they discover personality traits in themselves that are not in keeping with this image they will transfer these flaws onto other people and then focus on those flaws; exposing them in others whether they exist or not! In fact this is a sign that they are unable to achieve any self-insight; a classic sign of a narcissist. Their defense mechanism is rigid and will not allow anything to come through it; not even them!

5. Interpersonal Boundaries

The issue that follows pushing your flaws onto others and failing to acknowledge their own personality traits is that it becomes very difficult to establish the boundaries of their own existence and those of others. This lack of boundaries is also prevalent in their attitude to others; they assume others are there to serve them and assist them in their aims. They cannot imagine that these people have their own lives, hopes and dreams!

An extension of this is their ability to share inappropriate items; such as how they berated someone. They will not be aware of how their words may shock or offend others; they will be too busy bragging to worry about the response or whether they should be relating the facts. Their lack of boundaries is also likely to see those asking questions that are too intimate for the situation or their knowledge of the other person. This can be very upsetting and damaging to any relationship.

The lack of boundaries also extends to an inability to accept fault; they will borrow money, tools or promise you the earth and then blame you for not reminding them to return it to you.

6. Conversations

Someone suffering from NPD loves to hoard the conversation. In reality it is highly unlikely that you will get a word in edgeways. In fact, if you do manage to inject something into the conversation it should agree with their point of view; if it does not, your words will either be dismissed or they will take great pleasure in correcting you.

Should you or anyone else manage to say a few words; or even have a separate conversation then it is highly likely that the narcissist will interrupt and quickly bring the conversation back to themselves. There will be little interest in any other topic of conversation.

Conversations will generally revolve around them reciting a story; which you have probably heard before. It will be about an especially heroic incident; where they were the hero. Occasionally they may tell a story of when they failed at something; but even this will put them in a good light as they will be seen to be a victim of manipulation.

Their other favorite topic will usually revolve around name dropping; even if they just saw a famous person it can be turned into a story about their best friend the celebrity.

7. Breaking the Rules

A person with NPD loves to show others how important they are by breaking the conventional rules. This may mean cutting into the front of a queue or creating and breaking multiple appointments. Any action which will make them feel they are above the generally accepted norm will enforce the idea in their head that they are special. They may even go out of their way to create situations where they can break the rules.

8. Image

The image which is projected by someone with NPD is essential; it must say successful, important and better than you. This will often be shown by driving expensive cars, indulging in cosmetic surgery or in their exaggerated stories of where they have been and what they have done.

They are also keen to own the best items possible; they may purchase these items at incredibly discounts but they will never pass this information on; they like you to feel that they are incredibly successful and money is not an issue.

9. Charming

Despite their lack of boundaries and their obsession with themselves, a person with NPD is very aware of the usefulness of others in achieving their aims. When they need to be they can be exceptionally charming, feeding you just the right amount of compliments to make you feel good about yourself and life. In return you may find yourself doing what they want you to. Of course, once you have done their bidding they will lose interest in you straight away!

10. Negativity

Just as someone with a NPD will enjoy telling stories of their greatness they will also be happy to spread negative rumors and comments to both gain attention and leave others feeling insecure or unsure of their own sense of self-worth. This suits a sufferer as they look good and they are able to keep you close for when they need you again; it appeals to them on all sides of their personality disorder.

11. Social Media

Thus has been a gold mind for people who love to be adored. People are far enough away that they are rarely offended by the comments on any social media site. Someone with NPD can build a big following by posting perfect photos and comments; designed to attract a legion of fans that will all sing their praises and help them feel like the great leader they believe themselves to be.

12. Damage

As people with NPD do not have time for the feelings and thoughts of others they are quick to use someone and leave them behind. The result is a trail of carnage, people who have been taken in by them and had parts of their life destroyed. The trail will become more visible the longer the behavior goes unchecked.

Thus damage is fuelled by the inability of someone with NPD to place other people's values, interests or well-being above their own. This combines with the slightest interest from another person, and the accompanying boost to their self-esteem; to make it very likely that someone with NPD will cheat on their current partner.

13. Awareness

Perhaps one of the biggest signs that someone is a narcissist is that they have no awareness of it. You can chat to them about narcissism and its various traits and they will be unable to relate that to their image of themselves. This is why obtaining treatment can be so difficult; they do not know they need help! Of course if you realize the issue you may be able to choose to cut your losses and move on; however this may not be possible if they are a member of your family, a boss or if you really love them. At times, dealing with a narcissistic personality disorder requires you to flatter them to keep the peace.

It is important to note that not everyone with NPD will have all these traits; they may have all of them or just a few of them. The critical point is that they are very self-obsessed and that they are not aware they have an issue. This disorder can be exceptionally destructive to the lives of those who suffer from it and the people who interact with them. Obtaining the right help is essential to ensure the cycle of self destructive behavior can be ended and a sufferer can build lasting, meaningful relationships.

Chapter 7: Common Narcissistic Situations You May Encounter

Friendship Situations

The narcissistic platonic friend makes a fantastic first impression; she relies on charm and charisma to draw attention to her. She may have even managed to charm herself into a situation you would never have imagined shortly after meeting you, such as getting into a VIP section of a concert or managing to get a seat at a hot restaurant without a reservation. She exudes an air of confidence that attracts everyone's attention and uses that to her advantage. You initially feel so lucky that someone like her took an interest in you, especially if her reputation preceded her.

Over time, however, you begin to notice her penchant for turning every conversation and situation around to be about herself. This could be as innocuous as always being sicker whenever you are also sick or could be as over-the-top as being the maid-of-honor at your wedding and announcing that she is pregnant or newly engaged during the toasts. When attention is not on her, she may feign fainting or put herself into a vulnerable situation to get all eyes back on her.

She exaggerates her relationships to people she perceives as powerful, especially if it makes her look better or special. She appears outwardly successful in her career and has to have the best of the best, always getting the newest model of her phone or needing to have the best car out of her friends, even if it is out of her budget.

Her confidence comes with hypersensitivity to criticism, and you eventually become accustomed to this and may even find yourself specifically avoiding saying anything critical for fear of triggering her anger. You feel obligated to flatter or praise her just to keep her happy, and her presence always leaves you inexplicably annoyed and mentally drained. She may even drop you as a friend if you say something she does not like.

Whenever you need her, she is unavailable or has a much larger problem. If your mother has recently passed and you turn to her for comfort, you may find yourself trying to comfort her as she cries about how her own mother has a strange growth on her skin and she just knows it must be melanoma, and she is so afraid of losing her mother. She will constantly make your worst moments and fears about herself, and you will find yourself helping her when you need her the most.

Family Situations

Do you feel like you are dealing with a narcissistic parent? Most of our parents tend to be overbearing, but only a few cross over into the territory of pathological narcissism. This can quickly turn a beautiful relationship into an absolute nightmare. If your parent is a narcissist, then here are a couple of ways in which you can cope.

The first step is to start processing your emotions. You must try to understand that their behavior is not just "difficult,'" but it is quite abnormal. Usually, most of us like to work out any problems we face in a way that is amiable and agreeable. However, a person with NPD thrives on this unfair power play. If your parent has NPD or if you suspect that your parent has NPD, then you might have noticed that it is almost always "my way or the highway" thinking that's applicable. This is a sign of narcissism. If you start to see any of the following signs, then your parent is a narcissist:

- Acts like they are better than others and often lives in a fantasy world

- Tries to belittle or demean you

- Likes to get their way at all times and can even resort to using threats or intimidation to achieve that goal

- Takes credit for all the good you accomplished

- Expects you to bolster their fragile ego

- Expects constant praise and admiration from you and never reciprocates

- Conveniently shifts all the blame onto you when things don't go their way.

You must understand that it is not your fault, and the only one to be blamed is your parent. Make a list of all the actions that hurt you in the past, acknowledge the pain you endured, and realize that you did nothing to deserve all that pain. For instance, if your narcissistic parent constantly belittled you for as long as you can remember, give yourself a moment to feel sad or angry about it all. You have the right to feel bad but understand that you did nothing to deserve it. Take some time to grieve the loss of the kind of relationship you always wanted with your parent but never got. It can be rather upsetting when you realize that your parent was not the positive force in your life like he was supposed to and might never be also. Give yourself permission and the time to grieve this loss.

You must establish certain boundaries in your relationship with your parent. Make a list of all the things you want your narcissistic parent to stop doing. You might want your parent to stop subjecting you to the silent treatment, stop criticizing your appearance and the choices you make in life, stop threatening or intimidating you, stop blaming you when things go wrong, or a number of other harmful behaviors.

Once you have identified your boundaries, you must communicate the same to your parent. If you fail to communicate, it is highly unlikely that a narcissistic parent will ever come to this realization on his own. You must not only state your boundaries, but you must also establish certain consequences if your parent crosses those boundaries. For instance, you can tell your parent that you can no longer spend any time with him if he keeps criticizing you about everything that you say and do.

The next step is to interact with your parent. You must decide whether you want to continue the relationship with your parent or not. If you feel like spending time with your parent is doing more harm than good, it might be better to stay away from your parent. A narcissistic parent's intention of continuing a relationship might be to further his own needs and interests. Keep this in mind while deciding.

You must lower your expectations for the interactions you do have with your parent. A narcissistic parent can easily turn a pleasant conversation into something quite terrible. To protect yourself from being disappointed, the best thing to do is lower your expectations. The chances of being disappointed are quite low if you don't have any expectations. For instance, if you are meeting your parent for dinner, don't expect any warmth, encouragement, or other similar behaviors. Instead, expect that the parent will talk about his life, show little or no interest in your life, and possibly even by unpleasant to you. If you prepare yourself to expect all this, you will not be surprised if it goes better than what you had in mind. If it doesn't, then at least you will not be disappointed.

Keeps your calm while dealing with a narcissistic parent? It is essential that don't challenge your narcissistic parent. In such a situation, the usual response you might receive will be anger and some form of defensiveness. Instead, try to keep your calm even when your parent says unpleasant things. If you are expressing your feelings, use the word "I," because it will prevent your parent from perceiving that you were criticizing him. For instance, if your parent criticizes your career choice, you can say something like "I love to teach, and I am glad I chose this profession."

You can seek the support of your friends or other family members while interacting with your parent. It will help make you feel less vulnerable and will give you the strength to keep going. If the situation does get uncomfortable, then you must always have an exit strategy in mind. The simplest thing to do is put as much physical distance between yourself and your parent as you can.

You must learn to protect your feelings. Those with narcissistic tendencies can easily distort your self-image and your perception of yourself. Being subjected to constant criticism is bound to have this effect on you. It is essential that you know your true self. You must not let your parent's unrealistic perspective of you put you down. You can make a list of all your strengths and weaknesses so you can see for yourself that your parent's opinion about you is nothing but distorted.

If your parent tries to instigate a fight or tries to provoke you, you need to disengage immediately. A narcissist will try to control you by starting an argument. So, the best thing to do is immediately disengage, and this will prevent the parent from exerting any form of control over you. Try to change the subject if you can, if not, you can walk away from the conversation. If your parent doesn't give up and continues the unpleasant conversation, feel free to walk away. Remember that you don't owe your parents anything, and your mental peace must be your priority.

You need to surround yourself with people who treat you well and are positive. A parent with NPD can have a strong negative influence on you. So, it is essential that you spend most of your time with people who treat you well and accept you for who you are. You don't need any negativity in life, and it will do you good to keep this in mind.

Apart from this, you need to start taking good care of yourself. You must not neglect your self-care, especially when a negative person is sucking out all of your positivity. Take some time for yourself and work on building up your self-esteem.

Relationship Situations

If you have noticed that your partner displays most of the traits discussed in the previous section, then you probably are in a relationship with a narcissist. Here are a couple of ways in which being in a relationship with a narcissist can be stressful.

Most narcissists tend to find it rather difficult to ever love and accept them. Their inability to love and accept themselves makes it rather impossible for them to ever fully love others. It means that it isn't wise to expect unconditional love from your narcissistic partner. Narcissists are often self-absorbed, and this doesn't change even when they have a partner or are in a relationship. Your partner might never fully understand your needs and will instead be too focused on his needs and wants. Your partner's inflated self-image will make him believe that he can take everything else for granted, and this line of thought applies to your relationship as well. A narcissist believes that others are there to serve him, and he expects the same from you. So, don't be surprised if your narcissistic partner takes you for granted. If you are in a relationship with a narcissist, then you can forget about having an iota of control over your life. You will slowly lose the ability to control your views, opinions, choices, or any aspect of your life. Your partner will slowly but certainly control you and will start making decisions on your behalf. After all, a narcissist cannot even perceive that others can think differently from him. Not just that, but a narcissist truly believes he knows everything. A narcissist needs constant attention, and there is no limit to the amount of attention, praise, and appreciation he requires. You can expect a narcissistic partner to get jealous about the smallest of things, and he will also misinterpret your failure to pay attention (as he deems fit) as a sign of disinterest. It can lead to a point wherein your partner can accuse you of being callous and cold toward him.

Also, your partner will likely start to feel uncomfortable with your other healthy relationships like the bonds you share with your family members, colleagues, friends, and such. The loss of social life is one of the side effects of being in a relationship with a narcissist. A narcissist can never be truly happy, and the same applies to your narcissistic partner. There will be times when you feel guilty that you cannot make him happy. You might even start to think that you are not good enough for him or that you are the reason why he is unhappy. All these feelings, if left unchecked, can soon make you lose your self-worth.

At Work Situations

You might have come across at least one narcissist at your workplace. A narcissistic coworker is someone who does the following:

- Will take all the credit for your effort and hard work

- Belittles you in front of your colleagues and other coworkers

- Tends to blame you for all failed projects

- Usually gives you backhanded compliments or criticism veiled as compliments

- Is aware of all your weaknesses and is quite aware of how to exploit them

- Tries every trick in the book to sabotage your career

- Spreads vicious gossip about you and denies all responsibility when confronted

- Uses pressure or even coercion to get you to do something they want and tries to showcase their supposed "superiority" by putting you down

The modus operandi of a narcissist is to look good and be perceived as the best, even if it comes at someone else's expense. A narcissist can stoop to any level to make he look good in front of others. While everyone might be quite taken with a narcissist initially, eventually the charm will run out, and people will finally see the narcissist's manipulative ways. However, by that point it is quite likely the narcissist has done sufficient damage. So, how can you protect yourself while dealing with a narcissist at work?

You must make it a point to get everything down in writing. If you are ever given any oral instructions at work, ask the concerned person to send you the same through an email. The best defense available to you is proper documentation of what the narcissist said and when it was said. If you can get the email directly from the narcissist's ID, it will make things easier for yourself. If you receive any directions from the narcissist, you can make a note of the same. Try to maintain proper documentation with the exact date, time, and place of the occurrence and with as much verbatim as you possibly can. If you ever need to hire legal counsel later on this documented proof will come in handy.

Narcissists cannot stand the thought of others excelling or leaving them behind. This means that narcissists don't shy away from looking for ways to get you fired or even demoted at work. So, you must try not to give them that opportunity. As mentioned earlier, narcissists are quite adept at finding the weaknesses of others and then exploiting them. It means that the narcissists you are dealing with at work will try to do everything possible to understand your weak points. Once they know what these weaknesses are, it will certainly be used against you. For instance, let us assume that the narcissist knows you have two kids at home. If the narcissist ever feels injured, threatened, or even insecure about something you said or did, then he can make snide comments questioning whether you are a good enough parent or not. The narcissist will keep pushing your buttons to find what triggers you. So, don't give the narcissist this satisfaction. The simplest course of action is to ignore the narcissist.

It is quite unfortunate if a narcissist has ever targeted you. A narcissist tends to target those who do better than the narcissist or have some traits the narcissist desires but doesn't possess. If the narcissist feels that you are "better" than him, then you will become the target. Well, you must keep in mind that it isn't about you, and it is a manifestation of the narcissist's insecurities. Even though the behavior might not convey this, a narcissist's insecurities about his capabilities are what make him target others. So, it is time to realize that it is not personal, and this certainly makes it easier to walk away.

Indulging in office gossip is quite common; having opinions about other coworkers is common too. However, you must be careful about who you share your opinions with. Don't fall into the narcissist's trap of "so, what do you think of ____ (coworker)?" Regardless of whether your answer to that question was positive or negative, the narcissist will certainly find a way to twist your words and use it against you. The narcissist is an emotional predator capable of sensing when someone's hit a rough spot. If you are going through a rough phase in life, the worst thing you can do is share your troubles with a narcissist. All the information you give up can and will be used against you.

Perhaps the best but the most difficult thing to do is refuse all sorts of contact with the narcissist. If you don't want to get sucked into the narcissist's world of mental manipulation and deceit, then the best thing to do is avoid contact. If you cannot avoid the said narcissist at work, then limit your interaction to what is required and nothing more. Keep things as strictly formal and professional as you possibly can.

Apart from all these things, you must also be aware of your legal rights. If you feel like you are being mentally harassed or are scared for your safety, it is time to take some legal action. When in doubt, you can consult the legal team at your workplace or the HR manager. Please remember that you don't have to put with any form of harassment!

Chapter 8: How to Survive a Narcissistic Relationship

Relationships of all kinds with narcissists follow three stages: Love bombing, devaluing, and discarding. This predictable cycle is followed regardless of the type of relationship is forged with the narcissist; narcissists will repeat this with romantic partners, children, friends, and anyone else in their lives who accept it. Those who do not accept it are either demeaned and attacked or completely disregarded and dismissed. While the three stages are followed, narcissists' behavior changes somewhat depending on the kind of relationship and what is socially acceptable within those relationship's norms.

Signs You Are in a Relationship with a Narcissist

A romantic relationship with a narcissist begins perfectly. It feels like it is out of a storybook about true love, and for a good reason; both the storybook and the narcissist's persona are fictitious. The narcissist works hard to draw in his target, seeking to make the target fall hard and fast for the narcissist. This is accomplished through mirroring and love-bombing.

The narcissistic romantic partner may send flowers and love notes to work every day while constantly texting their target about how beautiful they are and how perfect the two of them are together. The romantic partner may invite their target on dates constantly and will push for the relationship to move at a much quicker pace than is typical, even if the target is uncomfortable with it. The narcissist will be more controlling than the target likes, but the target will justify this as being overly-protective or due to past trauma.

Over time, as the target becomes more attached to the narcissist, the narcissist's mask begins to crumble. First it may crack slightly, but eventually, it disintegrates, leaving the narcissist in all his glory, unmasked and unbearable while you find yourself too in love with the mask to leave its pieces on the floor without trying to salvage it. With the victim firmly attached to the narcissist, the narcissist finds he free to be himself. If he feels slighted in any way, he may lash out at the target, saying things that are hurtful or demeaning, or even yelling and intimidating the target into submission.

When in a narcissistic relationship, it is common to feel lonely, or as if you are unimportant, as the narcissist stops putting your desires first as soon as he feels you are firmly within his grasp. He no longer has to go through the effort of winning you over because you have already found yourself head-over-heels in love thanks to the intensely wonderful honeymoon period. He may move on to other tactics to keep you around, such as demeaning you or gas lighting you. You will be left with self-esteem as wounded as the narcissist's, but unlike the narcissist, yours can heal back into something healthy if given the self-care you need.

At the end of the relationship, the narcissist discards you; he may have moved onto a new source to feed his narcissistic supply, or he may have decided that the effort in maintaining you as useful is no longer worthwhile.

Is There a Future for a Relationship Touched by Narcissism?

We have covered a lot of information about the victim's future but what about the narcissist's future.

It isn't a nice picture if the narcissist won't get help. If they don't, it will be likely that they will just jump from one relationship to the next. If they do find a long-term relationship, their partner won't be really fulfilled and happy. They will more than likely just be putting up with the narcissist.

If during the duration of the narcissist's relationship they had children, the bad news is their children will probably develop narcissist behaviors since they were exposed to it through their growing years. Even though there isn't a definite answer to what causes narcissism, there are suggestions that experiences during childhood has firm links toward developing the disorder during their adolescent or adult years.

Narcissists are known to become bitter with time. This is mainly due to people coming into their lives and then leaving them and they can't figure out why. They will always put the blame onto someone else and will never see they had a role in them leaving. Most narcissistic traits get worse with age as they experience more things through their life.

You can see it is a very bleak picture and this is the sad truth about the narcissist's life. People will only stay around if they are treated nice. If they get treated like crap, they will eventually leave. Some might not get to that point but relationships with narcissists are usually empty and don't have respect and true love.

The biggest price any narcissist will pay for their actions with time will be loneliness and not ever knowing what a meaningful relationship really is.

The deepest and most meaningful relationship a narcissist will have will be with them.

Should We Blame Social Elements?

You almost know all there is to know about narcissists and the issues and traits that go with it. We also need to look at another area. Are social elements to blame for the increasing number of narcissists?

True narcissists are very rate but it is a term that we hear more and more. For this reason, narcissistic behaviors are more common now, so we need to find out why? Is it all the social pressures we have to deal with? Is it social media? Is it because we are pressured to own the best, look, the best, and be the best?

It is unfair to put the blame of narcissism at modern society's feet. It does make one wonder if it did have a hand in it. Social media makes us aware of the way other people live and look. The influences of social media tell us that if we want to be the best, we must look our best, and this means we have to use a certain product. We get bombarded with people constantly taking selfies and full body photos and then using filters and photoshop to change their appearance drastically. The majority of what we see just isn't real. Now, do you wonder why we have all these unrealistic expectation of what we should look like, what we should be, and what we need to aim for?

No one is completely sure what causes narcissism, so it is the things we are exposed to in life? Most of the narcissistic cases are thought to come from things we experienced during childhood, but what caused those experiences? What makes someone act a specific way? What makes someone create trauma to another human that can cause them to develop a certain personality disorder? It is hard to figure out, but you have to take into account all the possibilities.

We might not completely understand what causes narcissism, and there is a specific amount of stigma attached to it. If we try to be the best, it will be a constant, fruitless task. We should try to just be ourselves.

When talking about future generations, it is our responsibility to make sure our children are brought up to be happy just being who they are, without have to constantly compete to reach unrealistic goals. If we can do this, we are going to raise a generation of young people who are fulfilled, respectful, and well-mannered. These are great boosts toward avoiding trauma and personality disorders.

Chapter 9: The Narcissist and The Empathy

When it's Time to Leave

At this point, your partner must be willing to at least try to make some changes in their behavior in order to improve their own mental health and your relationship. If your partner is willing to do some of the work, then your relationship can be saved. But, if you have been engaging in the activities discussed previously in this book and your partner still does not see any problem with their behavior, there isn't much hope for an improvement. Unfortunately, as much as we want to believe that we can change another person, we cannot. You can change the dynamics on your end, which can improve the relationship for you, but in order for your partner to truly overcome their narcissistic traits, they have to put in some effort, too. This chapter will outline some of the things that your partner can do to improve their narcissistic tendencies. These techniques are the last step to turn a narcissist into a loving and attentive partner.

Identify the Maladaptive Behaviors that need to be changed

What types of behaviors does your partner see as maladaptive or problematic? This could come from a list that you make or that your partner understands to be true, or a combination of both. Once your partner acknowledges the inappropriate behaviors, he or she can begin to attack and alter them head-on.

Once you both know and understand the types of behaviors to work on, you can set up the positive and negative reinforcement system. Basically, if your partner does something positive to change their behavior, they should be rewarded somehow, and if they engage in one of the behaviors that you are trying to get rid of, a negative reinforcement (often called punishment) should be used like the "No Contact" principle. It works when, for instance, your partner gets abusive, and you distance yourself away from him or her to protect yourself as well as to cool things over. Your partner will eventually realize his or her mistake and will ask you to talk and deal with the problem. The punishments and rewards should be worked out between you both, and your partner has to be willing to commit to this. Many studies have shown that positive reinforcement works better than negative in the long term, so it makes sense to reward all small behaviors in a great way. If these rewards involve both of you, it could be a great way to strengthen your bond.

Practice Service to Others

People can learn to care for others. They have to choose to put the needs of another person before their own needs. If your narcissistic partner is willing to try this, it will be the first step to a loving partnership.

To do so, your partner should put aside one of their needs and do something for you no matter how simple or small it is. Whether that means running an errand that you usually do, making dinner for you, or taking care of one small thing so you don't have to do it, ask your partner to do something, anything for you. Start with something small, and over time, your partner will develop the ability to do more and more for you.

If your partner is willing to do these things for you, it is a good sign that they are willing to change. Talking about each other's needs and deciding what the boundaries are on both sides of the relationship is important. If your partner is amenable to do things for you, you, yourself, should be ready to do things for them as well, especially with regards to their mental health and stability. As we discussed earlier, you have the right to say no to unreasonable demands, but, in a loving relationship, you have to give as well. But first, it must be must be reasonable.

Your partner can learn that providing a service to others will benefit both of you and your partner can develop joy from seeing you happy, but it takes practice. Service to others is important to develop empathy for another person, which is the next step in the process.

Practice Empathy

Simply defined, empathy is the ability to put you in another person's place. By imagining how another person feels, you can relate to them better. The narcissist needs to be able to do this, and it is a skill that takes practice. You can facilitate this by explaining to your partner how you feel when they do a certain thing. As they begin to understand this, they will be better able to put themselves in the position of another. Once your partner can understand how another person feels, they will be more likely to help them.

Don't Take Life So Seriously

To someone with narcissism, not getting their way seems like a life and death situation. But examining what happens if the narcissist doesn't get their way can make it easier to understand that horrible things will most likely not happen.

The narcissist needs to remind themselves that they are not perfect and they do not have to be. They need to look for the humor in little things. As soon as they learn not to take life so seriously, humor can be found. And tomorrow, it probably won't even be that important. Once your partner realizes that even though yesterday seemed like a life and death situation, it's not the same as the present situation and so it will become easier to not take things so seriously, to laugh at their own mistakes, and to move forward in a more loving way. When everything is no longer about them and they face the fact that they cannot get everything they wanted and learn that it is not a crisis, things will get easier. They will learn to let go of these things and to move on more easily. Your partner will learn that they do not have to have control of everything. Life will not fall apart.

Practice Self-Compassion

This is especially true if your narcissist is the grandiose type, but it is more important to practice self-compassion rather than develop self-esteem. Your narcissistic partner already has plenty of confidence, and this is what makes them think they are entitled to everything they want and desire. Instead, fostering self-compassion will also help promote tenderness for other people. And, in the end, this is what will cause your partner to change their behavior, by understanding that everyone deserves love and respect. It starts with loving and respecting themselves.

To foster self-compassion, consider the three steps namely, developing self-kindness, understanding our common humanity, and practicing mindfulness.

Self-kindness is the simple idea that we should not beat ourselves up when something goes wrong. It means that when we talk to ourselves in our mind, it should be kind, rather than harsh. If you or your partner makes a mistake, what thoughts go through your mind? Do you berate yourself or do you try to comfort yourself? Most narcissists will berate themselves, and then lash out to try and make they feel better. Instead of lashing out at themselves, they should practice saying kind things in their mind. Remind yourself that everyone makes mistakes and that it's okay not to be perfect because no one is. Say nice things to yourself.

Second, realizing that everyone faces the same struggles will help to connect to that common bond that we call humanity. Everyone has imperfections. Everyone feels insecure at times and everyone has problems. When you practice self-compassion, you put yourself on the same level with everyone else around you. This is a necessary step for the narcissist. When they are able to do this, they can stop treating everyone else as if they are only meant to serve their needs. They will realize that they are part of a greater whole, not above it. This will make it easier for them to change their behaviors. This is the key realization to turn a narcissist into a loving human being; that everyone comes from the same place and has issues from various roots. No one's problems or ideas are more important than another's.

Lastly, the narcissist must learn to practice mindfulness which means keeping your thoughts in the present moment. It also means acknowledging your feelings as they happen and thus deal with them. By suppressing what one thinks and feels, it will cause emotional outbursts later. By dealing with them in the present moment, the narcissist will be less likely to act out in negative ways.

By working through these steps, the narcissist can be turned into a thoughtful and loving person. Self-compassion, when practiced regularly, will naturally transform into compassion for the world around them. It will need much effort and will take time. Doing these things is not an easy, but the benefits for both the narcissist, and you, as the partner, will be immensely gratifying.

Understanding Gas Lighting

Gas lighting comes from the movie of the same name that was released in 1944. This refers to a manipulation tactic some people use, especially the narcissist, to try and cause doubt in the minds of their victims. The way a person gaslights depends on the situation, but the main objective remains the same. They want to reinvent past events in order to make sure their errors or mistakes stay hidden.

In the example above, Margaret clear remembers that her mother spank her and her siblings. This was verified by the conversation she had with her brother, so she knew she hadn't made it up. When her mother noticed how good her granddaughter acted, she knew that Margaret's parenting was working, and that showed her choice of spanking wasn't the best discipline method.

With this in mind, Margaret's mother wanted to create distance between her and that discipline practice since it has become seen as harmful, ineffective, and unnecessary. She chose to claim she never did it, despite the fact Margaret and her brother remember having to face it as children.

With this example, the gas lighting seems relatively harmless and Margaret could just brush it off. But with narcissistic gas lighting, it becomes extreme and it can create serious doubt and it can even cause their victim to start questioning their sanity.

This is only one tactic that a narcissist will use in order to protect their image, not just how they appear in the present, but in the past as well. They have to make sure that they appear correct in every part of their life, so they strive to stay away from being branded for little mistakes even if they took place decades ago. Gas lighting allows them to sweep these mistakes under the rug while also hurting a person's sanity, which to them, means nothing.

Smear Tactic

If you start to notice that people distance themselves from you once you get out of the clutches of the narcissist, they have probably started a smear campaign. While politics typically hold the most popular smear campaigns, narcissists will sometimes use these same strategies.

Once you cut ties with a narcissist, they have realized something; you know who they truly are. This means that if you were to start exposing the narcissist for whom they really are, which likely isn't even a part of your plan, and then they are going to have to be carefully because their façade may start to crumble. This isn't something that they want to face.

What is a narcissist to do? They will use smear campaigns to stay a step ahead of them. They use the information they have about you and the relationship you had with them. They will make sure to talk with mutual friends before you to clarify the reasons why you two are no longer speaking. This will likely involve tweaking some information to make you out to be the bad guy.

It's important to note that a narcissist is not going to settle for just mentioning a couple of nasty things. They looking to completely destroy your reputation and credibility. This ensures that you would have a very hard time trying to convince your friends what you really experienced. You come off as unreliable, and they keep the friends and their reputation.

If the narcissist chooses to do a smear campaign, it can leave you without anybody to turn to. Some gossip and rumors can be so bad that it could harm your job and other relationships. Keep in mind, they never really cared about you to begin with, so don't be surprised if they become somebody unrecognizable and start sharing absolute lies about you and the things you have done.

Abuse by Surrogate

The one thing that a narcissist never runs out of is people. People gravitate towards them for the same reason you did. Unfortunately, if somebody chooses to cross a narcissist, they will find themselves dealing with attacks from the rest of their posse.

This is something that you could refer to as abuse by surrogate. This will start the moment you upset them. Their need to discourage and shame will hit full force, and they are going to make sure that you feel their unhappiness for what you have done to them. They will also take things a step further and make sure they really hit where it hurts. This is where other people will step in.

Narcissists, as we discussed above, will start to talk to other people in their circle about you. They will convince them that you are the one at fault, and that you must be taught a lesson. The interesting thing is that they won't actually say those exact words. It looks more like brainwashing by making the other people believe certain lies and to encourage them to act on certain ideas without instruction.

Here's an example:

Damito is the middle child. Her sisters are A+ students and they bring home impeccable report cards and they get a lot of praise from their teachers. Damito is just an average student. While she may not get the grades her siblings do, she does come home with decent grades. She is by no means failing.

One day, though, she does fail an exam and her mother loses her mind. She reprimands her, says she's lazy, and that she is worried about her future. She says that her performance isn't going to get her anywhere in life, and it upsets her to say that Damito isn't going to able to achieve what her sisters do.

Damito is sent to her room after being reprimanded in front of the family at dinner. She cries and sulks in her room for the rest of the night. Meanwhile, her sisters are still at the dinner table, and her mother continues to complain.

She praises Damito's sisters. The great grades give meaning to the long hours she spends at work to be able to afford their schooling. The children feel happy and loves by their mother's words, and the thank her for all of the effort she puts in to make sure that they can get the best education.

While they are talking, she calls Damito ungrateful, saying she doesn't deserve to get the same opportunities as her sisters because she doesn't appreciate what her mother does. She goes on to tell them that they shouldn't associate with people like Damito because they can be bad influences and cause them to lose sight of the things that are important.

Before their conversation comes to an end, she says that she still has to work hard and hope for the best, even if some of them don't appreciate what she does. The end their conversation and the kids go to bed.

The following day, Damito gets up and head to the kitchen for breakfast to find that all of the food has been eaten. "You got up late, so you don't get food," her older sister tells her rudely. During the day Damito is showered with the same harsh and negative energy from her sisters who seem to be trying to avoid her.

This makes her feel ashamed and alone for what she did. This causes her to approach her mother and apologizes for being ungrateful for all of the work she has done. She "accepts" her daughter's apology, but she stays cold towards her daughter in the next few days, which her sisters mimic.

Can you see the problem in this scenario?

First, it's important to see the aggravation. What did Damito do to get this kind of treatment from her mother, and then her sisters? A single failed test. For the majority of us, one bad grade isn't a reason to get this upset. In fact, most parents would let this slide with saying nothing more than, "do better next time."

However, since Damito's mother is a narcissist, she views any type of failure as completely unacceptable. Her children are an extension of her, so if they have any shortcomings, it is completely unforgivable because if reflects badly on her.

She made a point of reprimanding Damito in front of her sisters. This shows her anger and imparts shame because everybody else gets to hear and see her receiving this punishment.

Next, once Damito leaves, her mother continues to talk with her sisters. She starts out praising them, telling them how proud she is of them being top students. Of course, it's easy to infer that they only perform so well because of the pressure from their mother and not because they actually want to do well.

By talking to Damito's sisters, she can trick them into feeling the same animosity towards her, who didn't even do anything malicious to anybody in the family. Her sisters and her mother don't have a real reason to be upset with her because the grade she gets doesn't affect any of them. However, since her mother used the tactic divide and conquers, they fell connected to her and thus become aligned with her by mimicking how she feels.

What happens next? They will unknowingly emotionally abuse Damito by giving her the cold shoulder. They distance their self from her and treat her like a pariah. This causes Damito to feel the brunt of her "mistake" and has no choice but to apologize, even though she shouldn't have to.

Abuse by surrogate can be hard to handle because it causes the victim to feel isolated. They start questioning themselves and they may even begin to believe their abuser had a good reason to treat them so badly. What's more, they feel the added pressure from the "mob" which complicates their internal battle. If everybody is mad at me, then I must have done something wrong.

What is important to remember is that just because several people believe something, doesn't make it true. When you are at the brunt end of abuse by surrogate it can cause you to start questioning your validity and integrity but staying strong and deciding to believe the truth will help you to be less affected by their abuse and disapproval.

Dealing with Emotional Abuse

If you or your partner find these steps quite difficult, it can be useful to seek professional help.

A therapist or counselor can be an impartial guide to following these steps, can provide essential insight that you both missed, and can make sure that the two of you are not seeking to hurt each other, even unintentionally. Although not necessary, a therapist can be a valuable asset in the quest of turning your narcissist partner into an unselfish, loving partner.

It is my sincere hope that you and your partner are both willing to put the work necessary in your relationship to improve it. By following the techniques laid out in this book, you can have the person you love turn into a thoughtful, unselfish partner. But they, too, have to be willing to do the work. Remember, you cannot force someone to change. You can change how you act, but if your partner is not willing to engage in the work laid out in this chapter, there is only so much you can do to improve your relationship. But, working together, you and your partner can accomplish miraculous things. You can get the loving partner you want and he or she can learn to deal with life and relationships more effectively.

Chapter 10: How Can You Help a Narcissistic Person?

The tendency toward narcissism is quite common, and it is present in all of us. At times, you might not know if someone has a particularly high degree of narcissism until you are deeply involved with them. Only then do you realize that all the traits you were attracted to be narcissistic qualities you cannot stand anymore. You might have a parent, a sibling, a partner, or even a friend who exhibits narcissistic traits and you may be forced to deal or work along with them. It doesn't mean narcissists are unlovable; it merely makes it rather difficult to love them at times. People with high levels of narcissism might be fun, good at what they do, and quite charismatic and charming. If you have a say in the matter, you might like the idea of reforming narcissists instead of cutting off all ties with them. No two individuals are alike, and likewise, all narcissists aren't the same. So, the way you decide to handle a narcissist in your life will depend on the type of narcissist you are dealing with.

Vincent Egan, a psychologist associated with the University of Nottingham, compiled data from an online sample of over 800 participants in 2014. The main objective of the study was to understand whether a relationship exists between NPD and wellbeing. The findings of previous researchers show a difference between vulnerable and grandiose types of narcissists. A vulnerable narcissist's façade of self-absorption and self-centeredness are a means of disguising his weaknesses. A grandiose narcissist on, the other hand, truly does believe in his own superiority and greatness. Such narcissists might be as good as they seem to believe they are.

You Cannot 'Save' Anyone

These are two types of narcissists, but the narcissists with grandiose narcissism might share more similarities with the traits exhibited by the dark triad. The dark triad refers to certain traits, which include the inclination to seek special treatment (narcissism), to be callous toward others and exhibit insensitivity (psychopathy), and a tendency to manipulate others (also known as Machiavellianism). Those who exhibit traits of Machiavellianism and narcissism are the ones who can truly annoy you. The same was pointed out by Egan and his team. Those with such traits can make it rather difficult to live with them and might also make it difficult for you to attain your goals. Machiavellian narcissists are quite adept at showcasing their superiority while stepping all over the feelings and opinions of others. The research also shows that a narcissist can be happy, but it is less likely to be a happy manipulator or a happy psychopath.

The participants in the study conducted by Egan and others were asked to rate themselves on a personality test, which provided ratings on the five factors or the traits of emotional stability, extroversion, conscientiousness, openness to experience, and agreeableness. They were also asked to rate themselves on the traits described by the dark triad. The subjective wellbeing of the participants was measured using two scales, one that measured happiness and the other related to their satisfaction with life.

Once the scores were analyzed based on these scales, the team of researchers managed to identify four types of narcissists. The two distinct categories were the vulnerable and the grandiose narcissists. The other two categories consisted of people who were identified by their generalized happiness, and the remaining category consisted of individuals who showcased overall happiness along with low scores of narcissism. By comparing the two types of narcissists, Egan and his team of researchers discovered that those who exhibited the traits of a grandiose narcissist were more inclined toward being happy, extroverted, and emotionally stable. On the other hand, the vulnerable narcissists were the ones who were less emotionally stable, less agreeable, and exhibited traits of extreme levels of manipulation and psychopathy.

Keeping all these things in mind, let us take a look at the ways you can handle your emotions while dealing with narcissists.

The first step is to understand the kind of narcissist you are dealing with. Vulnerable narcissists are incapable of feeling good about them. Grandiose narcissists are quite expressive when it comes to their emotions. So, you might not even be aware that such narcissists are getting in your way. If you are trying to accomplish something, then having a grandiose narcissist in your corner will be quite helpful. However, the one thing you must make sure is that their goals are in alignment with your goals.

You need to acknowledge the annoyance or irritation you experience. Narcissists can be rather antagonistic and will get under your skin. If you are trying to accomplish something, and one person always seems to interrupt your efforts or tries to shift the focus onto himself, then it will help if you can identify where your annoyance is stemming from. Once you can do this, you can get the necessary strength to put a stop to it all and keep going. If you don't acknowledge your annoyance, you will never be able to deal with it properly.

You must understand what prompts the narcissists to behave the way they do. Narcissists not only like but they also need to make themselves feel good about themselves, and this can translate into them behaving in a manner that is sneaky and even demoralizing. They might question your authority and intentions to create trouble. Once you understand that their acts are guided by deep-seated insecurity, you will be able to give them the necessary reassurance to help them calm down and concentrate on important things. Too much reassurance can fuel their egocentric ways, but given the right amount, it can help them settle down and focus on the task at hand.

You must understand the context. Narcissism is such that some circumstances might trigger an individual's insecurities more than other instances. For instance, consider a situation wherein a woman was passed over for a promotion she desired, and now she must continue to keep working with the person who got the job she wanted. Her insecurities are bound to worsen, and it can make her spiteful and even vindictive. If you have ever worked with such a person or known someone like this, then please remember that the circumstances helped shape the traits exhibited by the person you must now deal with.

You must hold onto positivity, especially when you are handling narcissists who derive pleasure from the misery of others. When such narcissists see others suffer, it merely fuels their ego and eggs them on. Even if you feel disturbed, try not to let it show and don't give the narcissists the satisfaction that they managed to get under your skin. If you can do this, then it will eventually discourage the narcissists.

You must not lose your focus. Please don't get derailed from concentrating on your goals even when the narcissists try to steal the spotlight. You don't have to pay heed to everything the narcissists say, regardless of how much they want your attention. You must strike some balance between moving ahead and attaining your goals and helping ease the narcissists' anxiety and insecurities. You must realize that you must not put your life on hold to help alleviate the narcissists' insecurities.

Hold onto your sense of humor. You can call narcissists' bluffs by either ignoring them or meeting them with a sense of humor once in a while. However, don't be cruel while doing this. Instead, you can try to gently point out that the narcissists' behavior is inappropriate and egocentric. Do this with a smile on your face. This is a great way to deal with a grandiose kind of narcissist who might take the rebuttal in an instructive manner and might even find it entertaining.

You must understand that the narcissist might need help. Most narcissists tend to have a rather low level of self-esteem and suffer from feelings of extreme inadequacy. So, it is important to recognize their need for help.

Are Narcissists Dangerous?

As unfortunate as it is, there is a certain point at which a relationship becomes too toxic. No matter how much you may love the person, it is time to end the relationship and move on so that you can find real happiness in your life. While milder forms of the narcissistic personality disorder have the potential to be dealt with and resolved; severe forms are often too far gone and the risk of staying with the person become too great.

Below are some warning signs that it may be time to get out of a toxic relationship with a narcissistic partner. If after all this, you are still unsure, you should consult a psychiatrist specializing in narcissistic personality disorder to discuss your relationship and seek his or her professional opinion about what you should do.

The Key Warning Signs

- Pathological lying: because narcissists often use manipulation in order to get the admiration they desire, they will often tell any lie they think will help them achieve that end goal. If your partner is lying consistently about important and trivial things, your relationship has no foundation in anything real. You cannot trust anything that they say, including when they tell you that they love you. If you cannot trust your partner, you have nothing to build on. This can approach dangerous extremes especially if your partner is having affairs. You will be at an increased risk for STDs if they sleep around and do not use protection.

- Fits of anger or rage: narcissists have a hair trigger. The slightest criticism or disagreement can spark an onslaught of abusive language and anger. When the fit of rage is over, your partner will act is if nothing had happened. He or she will show no sign of remorse and if they do apologize, it will not be genuine. It is unhealthy for you to endure such emotional abuse and it can have major consequences in the long term. In some cases the verbal abuse can even become physical. Whether or not it has reached that point in your own relationship, it is time to get out if you are experiencing any form of abuse from your partner.

- Manipulative behavior: the person you love should not be doing anything to manipulate you. Period. Strong relationships are built on honesty and trust. You should be able to trust that the things your partner says and does for you are genuine and come from a place of love and not a place of narcissistic selfishness. This manipulative behavior can sometimes fool you into believing that your partner does genuinely care about and love you but you have to try to look past what you want to see and find out what really lays at the root of your partner's actions. If you find yourself doing things you would not normally do or doing things that later make you feel guilty or unhappy just because your partner wants you to; this is manipulation. No matter how much your partner may say he or she loves you; people do not manipulate the people they love. You should never be forced into doing something you are not comfortable doing for a loved one.

- Feeling obligated: It is a bad sign if you are doing things (like staying in the relationship) simply because you feel obligated to or fear the consequences of not doing them. In a healthy relationship, partners do things for each other because they love each other and because they genuinely wish to see the other person happy. Of course, there are certain responsibilities and duties to uphold in the maintenance of a relationship. But this is different than a sense of obligation. If you are worried that your partner will abandon you or experience a fit of rage unless you do exactly what he or she wants; this is a sign that you are not doing it because you genuinely wish to see him or her happy but, rather, because you do not wish to see him or her unhappy.

- Feeling afraid: Just as you should not do things for your partner out of a sense of obligation, you should also not do things out of a sense of fear. Healthy relationships should provide a safe space for both your partner and you. Being with the person should make you feel secure and happy. Feelings of fear should not ever enter the equation. You should not have to fear the person you love.

- Becoming isolated from others: narcissists are often extremely jealous. Your partner will become more and more controlling of who you spend your time with and how much time you spend outside of his controlling reach. You will find yourself spending more and more time at home and growing distant from your friends and social circle. This isolation can make you feel unnecessarily dependent upon your partner; as if leaving him or her will mean being utterly alone. Becoming isolated from your social support is dangerous. If your partner does begin abusing, your friends and family may have no idea what is going on. So if you begin to notice that you have grown apart from your friends and family because of your partner, you need to leave. Your loved ones will be there for you. You will not be alone.

- Ignoring your own needs: if keeping your partner happy means neglecting or wholly ignoring your own needs, this is not healthy. A relationship should be about give and take with both partners providing emotional support for each other. Someone who loves you will not require you to put aside your own needs in order to appease them because they will have genuine concern for your needs just as you have for theirs. Never allow your own needs and desires to go unmet for the sake of your partner. This sort of relationship cannot end in happiness and will become extremely emotionally draining.

Chapter 11: Dating After Leaving a Narcissist

Getting back the control of your life after years of abuse might seem like a difficult thing to do. But with the right guidance and using the right tools, you can effectively regain your control and find happiness again.

Yes, you have been abused. Yes, you have allowed this narcissist into your life for years. It will take quite a long time to regain control of your life after years of being isolated, stalked and monitored. But following the subsequent ways, you can remove the marks of abuse and get back to your original self as explained in chapter 9 above. These steps will help you to hold the control of your life and take revenge against the narcissist as discussed in chapter 12.

Get the Negativity Out of Your System

Like it or not, there is a whole lot of negativity within your system by the time you are parting with a narcissist. This toxicity accumulated as you tried to appease them and in trying to make the relationship work. You tried to understand the narcissist as they took advantage of you more and more. It is now time to let go of all that darkness and allow space for your life to take shape again. Some of the things you can do to get this negativity out include journaling or sharing your story with a friend, or even engaging a therapist. Talking out the story is so helpful, especially when it is with a listening partner since it helps in organizing your confused thoughts into place. Also, it helps to empower you since you can finally be honest with yourself. Also, you can engage in mind and body exercises such as yoga or dancing. This helps to discard the toxicity and clears your mind to accommodate positivity.

Compile A List of The Controlling Incidents You Have Experienced

Although it might seem trivial, compiling the experiences of control and abuse helps you realize what you have been through and appreciate your growth - the fact that you will not allow yourself to be in such a situation again. Such remembrance gives you pride in your bravery of being able to leave such and look forward to a more rewarding life. You appreciate that you can now live as a free person and you cannot allow yourself to fall back in the abusive relationship.

Practice Listening to Your Inner Self

Your inner voice is the best tool you will ever have in dealing with any situation. It shows you how best you can do things and it never lies. Even amidst great pain and desperation, your inner voice can show you how to find your way out. The major reason why the narcissist was able to manipulate you was that they worked on the external stimulants of your brain, which in turn messed your internal stimulants as argues Morf,

Horvath and Torchetti (2011). They were fulfilling their selfish motives by controlling how your brain responds to things. However, listening to your inner voice will help you make out a situation and you can learn when to move ahead, hold back or reject things being said to you. It will guide you in your newly acquired life, one in which you are free, and you understand yourself much better. It will help you to never fall for a toxic person again.

Organizing Time and Space

It is good to have a clean and organized space since this allows you enough time to absorb everything that comes your way. When your space is full of clutter, you feel overwhelmed because it registers in your mind that you have a lot to do. As aforementioned, DE cluttering allows you to organize your space and remain with only the things that matter to you. You will find that your brain will respond positively to living in an ordered place. You will feel more settled and you are energized to face every new day. Also, clutter obscures your mind and your thinking. You can establish a good daily routine where your most significant tasks are allocated to the time of the day that you tend to be most active.

Connect with Family and Friends

As noted, narcissists usually isolate their victims from their loved ones and friends. They no longer understand you and they may even think that you hate them. They have judged you countless times because your attitude towards them has changed. There could be some of them who have tried to tell you that you are not okay in your relationship, but you have always denied their sentiments in the attempt to defend your narcissist partner, who has already conditioned you to support them against all forms of attack. Since you have been dependent on the narcissist for all your social contact needs, you find it difficult to associate with people. The truth is, however, that your loved ones are always eager to reconnect with you and spend time and share with you.

Be Patient: Take Your Time

The worst mistake you can commit is to judge yourself and think that you are not making fast progress regarding getting out of the pit and forgetting about your narcissist. You should not be hard on yourself. Instead, you should understand that healing takes time to be effective. Also, everyone needs different amounts of time to be able to get over something. Based on the depth of your abuse or length of the toxic relationship, you might need more or less time to heal.

There is no time limit on healing. Remember, your abuser has already separated you from your most precious people and hobbies. They conditioned you into feeling lost and lonely without them. Therefore, healing might take time and it is upon you to be kind on yourself and be patient as you heal. Most importantly, do not jump right into another relationship. This will obscure your thinking and deny you time to heal. Consequently, you will carry the burden right into the next relationship and it will not be healthy.

Acknowledge What Has Been and Forgive Yourself

You might be tempted to beat yourself up for allowing such a toxic person to be in your life for such a long time. However, true healing and regaining power entails accepting what has been that you have associated yourself with a highly toxic person, who has consciously hurt you. Accept that you have been tricked and abused. Trying to please them and showing them that you understood them, denied you the chance to identify the red flags. Also, they used your strengths against you: that you were caring, that you had a good job, that you were highly organized, open to ideas, and that you were financially stable. You never deserved this, and it was wrong of them to abuse you.

After acknowledging this, know that it was not your fault and forgive yourself. Forgiving yourself is the most important thing you need to do right now. No matter how much time, energy, wellness, and cash you have lost, that is in the past. You have to forgive yourself and move forward successfully. It does not matter why you stayed for so long, it does not matter why you were fooled. It already happened. So, forgive yourself.

Seek to Acquire Knowledge: Do Self-Inquiry

It seems so difficult to make sense of the abuse you have been through and what to do after this. For such a long time you have only learned to see the world through the perspective of your abuser. You are now confused and are wondering where to begin. Seek to be knowledgeable about emotional wellness. There are a myriad of articles and online courses that you have access to and that which can help you in this.

Knowledge is power, and enhancing your power never goes out of fashion.

Shift Your Focus

Because you have been abused for a long period it is easy to find your mind moving back to these thoughts. These are aspects of trauma and cognitive dissonance and are a hindrance to proper recovery. The reason why your mind may keep on pushing you back there is it wants to comprehend certain things and process related emotions. You should not entertain these thoughts about the past but capitalize on the present. You may find yourself making one step forward and two steps backward. Train your mind to be in the present and the future you have chosen to make for yourself. To boost your motivation in this endeavor you need to resurrect your dreams and this time let them be magnificent. Remember the dreams and things you wanted for yourself before being drawn to a narcissist; think about how bad you wanted them and boost your desire to achieve them. This is what it means to shift your focus to look forward and change your status from that of a victim to a hero in your life. Even though you have been through pain, after healing you may be surprised by the self-loving person - aware, whole and integrated - you have become.

Chapter 12: The Future for a Narcissist Who Refuses Help

If you do choose to leave your narcissistic family, friend, or partner, there are some things you should know about after that happens.

It really is simple, a narcissist isn't going to shrug their shoulders and say: "okay, see you later," and allow you to walk away without anything else happening. They will probably go back to their best behavior to get you back.

They do this for one reason and that is because they hate to be rejected and they take it very badly. If you leave a narcissist, you are rejecting them, and it doesn't matter how you were treated. They won't see all the manipulation and abuse that they did to you. According to them, you were treated like a queen or king. They will view your walking away and it is going to make them extremely angry or cut into the depths of their self-conscious. You should do one of the following next:

- They will get resentful and angry. They will bombard you with posts on social media, texts, messages and calls about how they are better without you and before they hang up they will call you every name under the sun.

- They could be the epitome of charm again and begin reminding you of all the good times you had together.

If you realize the first one is happening, ignore them and block them every way possible. This is just their pride taking over. They see you rejecting them. They view it as you are making a horrible mistake. They are trying to turn the tables on you. You can see through all their scandals. Block them any way possible; their phone number, on social media; don't go to any places that they frequent, go stay with family or friends for a week or so if you are worried they might show up at your place. They will eventually get bored and tired of no response from you.

The second point is also common and this is the way most people who are in a narcissistic relationship go back to the narcissist again and again. The best answer here is to be firm and keep in mind why you left them. If you can stay with your support group that would be the best thing you could do. These people are going to remind you about all the bad things when your resolve is waning and it are going to at times. Yes, you had some great times, and you were with them for reasons. If you are a victim of gas lighting, then you might not be sure what your next step should be since you will still be suffering from the effects of emotional abuse. Your family and friends will hold you firm but you will still need to stay firm and still block their numbers and on all social media sites. The less contact you have with them, the easier it is going to be to move forward.

What Should You Expect

- Silence eventually

- Begging

- Insults

- Pleading

- Blame games

- Bargaining

If you think you are free and clear once the silence begins, think again. If they spot you in town soon afterward, they are going to plead and bargain with you. Getting away from them will take time but it is a process you will be glad you started.

Dating Again

After you have gotten over the "getting rid of the narcissist" process, your future will look brighter. You have to give yourself time to grieve for the "dead" relationship, and whatever you do, don't jump right into another relationship to try to get over the narcissist. If you don't deal with all that has happened, you are risking your future. Most people who have gotten out of a narcissistic relationship are so traumatized by what happened during the relationship that they don't want to get near anyone else again. When a new person begins to show the smallest inkling of something that seems like narcissism, they will run.

The truth is that everyone has signs of narcissism every now and then, but this doesn't mean we are true narcissists. Everyone can lack empathy at times, we could belittle others without meaning to a couple of times, and we can act in horrible ways. The difference between us and a narcissist is that we apologize and see our mistakes, a narcissist won't. Don't make a mistake of labeling everybody with the same tag.

The best way to get your feet back in the dating pool after getting out of the narcissistic relationship is to begin slowly. Here are some tips to help you:

- Take some time to just "be". Don't try to do things. Don't try to feel things. Don't push yourself. Take time to be by yourself and unpack the events and finally deal with them. If you need someone else's opinion or to find professional help, this is the time to do it.

- Focus on yourself. Now is the time to find things you enjoy doing and be nice to you. You have spent a long time with someone who was constantly unkind to you. You have probably forgotten how to pamper yourself and enjoy it. Find something you have always wanted to try. Take a night class, go to movies with friends, spend the weekend being lazy, go for a walk in the park, eat your favorite foods, or read that book you've wanted to for a long time.

- Think about your health. After you have focused on yourself, now pay attention to your health. Have a healthy mind and body are the best revenge ever. You really shouldn't be thinking about revenge, but being a better you after you've had bad experiences will feel great. Challenge your mind, stay away from stress, get lots of sleep, get some exercise, and eat healthier foods. You will soon realize how stronger you are feeling.

- Start enjoying your life again. When you begin to feel better, and it might take some time, just begin to enjoy your life. Don't think about dating, and don't try to meet anyone new. If it does happen, let it happen. There will be plenty of time for that later.

- Once you are ready, just be open to the possibility. The main point is to meet somebody who will be worthy of your attention and time. Somebody who will give you what you didn't have before. You don't need anyone who can heal or complete you. If you think you are ready, just be open to meeting people but don't put any importance on it. People who have gotten out of narcissistic relationship might be needy since they are desperately trying not to let it happen again. If you can follow these steps and put importance on building yourself back up, this shouldn't happen to you.

- Don't think that everybody is going to act like your ex. If you do find somebody and decide to begin dating, don't put them in the same boat as your ex. This is extremely important. True narcissists are extremely rare and you need to remember this. It is very unlikely that you will meet someone else who is a narcissist twice in one lifetime. Yes, it might be possible that you will meet somebody who will act a tad bit narcissistic occasionally; they aren't a true narcissist and won't bring the same problems into the relationship.

- Recognize the signs. Don't run away at the first sign of a problem. Hold your requirements for understanding and respect at the top of your list. If anyone begins to treat you horribly, address the problem and stand firm before you walk away. If living through a narcissist relationship teaches you anything, it will be that you aren't going to let the same thing happen again.

If you are thinking that you won't ever try to date again, I am fine being by myself, it is time to ask yourself why you are feeling this way. Do you really not want a relationship and you want to be alone, you want to travel, or reconnect with friends you let slip away? Are you just saying it because you are scared of being hurt again?

Some people really don't want another relationship and this is perfectly fine, given it is for the correct reasons. If you are just staying away from romantic connections because you are afraid, this is something you need to address very early. You might find your feelings will change with time but remaining closed off to connections just because your past is clouding your judgment is going to hurt you more in the long run.

You must remember you deserve to be loved and it doesn't matter what you were forced to believe in the past.

Chapter 13: Are Modern Social Elements to Blame?

People who have a NPD are not generally aware of the issue and, as such, will not be able to see the effects this disorder has on their life. In fact, many of the people who come in contact with such a person will also fail to notice this as they will be taken in by the charm of the sufferer and then left behind when they are no longer useful. They may feel bitterness or regret for their decision to be involved with the person but they are unlikely to have been around long enough to realize that they have a personality disorder. This is actually part of the defense mechanism of somcone with NPD; an unconscious way to prevent people from getting to close and discovering the sufferer's secret. It falls to those who do know the sufferer for a long time; usually family and childhood friends, to bring up the issue; they can see the effects on their everyday life:

• Oblivious

People with NPD are generally oblivious to the
affect their actions have on those around them.
They may show some concern whilst someone is
useful for them to achieve their goals; after they
have been achieved they will move onto the next
thing. Disregarding people and the emotional hurt
it causes is not actually a callous act; they are
simply incapable of realizing the harm they do;
they are too busy protecting themselves and
aiming for their goals. It falls to the others in their
life to note how often they leave this trail of
damage behind and to help pick up the pieces.

• Relationships

Someone with NPD fails to form lasting
relationships; they are likely to have many short
term relationships but will be unable to commit to
one for the long term. The break up usually
happens when the partner fails to agree with them
on a specific issue. The issue can be small or big
but the person with NPD will not be able to accept

or understand why their partner does not agree with them. They will move on without a backward glance.

This, sadly, means that the majority of people with NPD do not get to experience the beauty of a deep and meaningful relationship with anyone or anything. In many ways they can be said to go through life with blinkers on; missing so much on the way. Because they shut themselves down they miss out on so many emotional experiences which can never be recaptured. In this sense someone with NPD needs to have compassion.

• Opportunities

Anyone who has NPD will miss out on a host of opportunities; these may even be things which will lead them to the success and fortune they desire! They will miss out as they will be unable to deviate from their chosen path. They belief that they know the best way to go and, as such, they will not choose a different path, no matter how good this alternative may appear to be. Without help, someone with a NPD is simply moving through life as a shell; so busy trying to make the right impression that they miss all the best opportunities.

If you choose to engage in a relationship with someone suffering from NPD, then the following tips should help you to build a future together while they receive professional treatment. Of course, you may not choose to have a relationship with someone, but if you love them you have no choice:

• Realize there is an issue

It will be likely that you start to blame yourself for the problems in your relationship. You may not be aware of NPD or even contemplate it as an option. However, if you start to study the behavior of your partner and compare it to the information in this book you will realize that you are dealing with someone who has a narcissistic personality disorder. You will then be able to do something about it!

• Stop encouraging the behavior

It will often be easier to give in and agree with your partner to stop the arguments. You may even flatter them a little to keep them happy. However, in the long term this will not help them or you. You must be strong enough to stand up to your partner and help them on the path to recovery.

• Boundaries

Living with a narcissist can be difficult even for the most patient and giving person in the world. The most important goal is to establish which needs are genuine and which are not. Armed with this knowledge you will be able to set boundaries regarding what you will and will not do. You will need to remind yourself of these boundaries daily and stick to them; if you give even a little you will find your partner demanding more and more.

• One-sided conversations

As already mentioned, people with NPD are expert at steering the conversation back to them, their needs and their achievements. The majority of conversation will revolve around them unless you choose to prevent this. The best way to stop this is to place a time limit on how long you are prepared to indulge in a conversation which focuses entirely on them. Once the time is up stop the conversation or walk away; if you do not you will be forever listening to their rants about themselves.

• Avoid self-blame

Anyone suffering with NPD will be reluctant, if not find it impossible, to acknowledge their own flaws. If they are in a relationship it is a very likely that they will project their flaw onto you; this will avoid them having to confront the issue themselves. They will then portray you as the hurtful one and, over time, you can even start to believe it yourself! You're frustration may well boil over although this may be turned against you as your partner states that it is you who has an issue and not them!

It is important to see this for what it is right at the start and avoid being drawn into it emotionally in the first place. If they attempt to project their flaw onto you it is time to tell them you are not playing that game; feel free to walk away of you need to.

• Avoid angry confrontations

The last line of defense for someone with NPD is anger. It is at this point they have lost control and there is a real risk of them lashing out. The aim of this may even be to get you to lose control so that the blame can be placed at your feet. It is essential to walk away as soon as the anger starts to rise; this will ensure your partner knows you have no interest in playing their games.

• Leave if you have to

Despite your best efforts you may find that your partner makes no effort to improve themselves or build your relationship. It is important to know when enough is enough; staying in a relationship with someone suffering from NPD can lead to emotional and even physical abuse. This can happen if the controls you attempt to put in place do not work and the narcissistic gradually wears you down and you lose your own feeling of self-worth. This pain and hurt can then be carried into future relationships making it difficult to commit to a long term relationship.

If you are in a relationship with someone suffering from NPD you must decide as early as possible how far you are prepared to take the relationship if they do not improve. When you reach this point you must be strong enough to walk away, ending the relationship before it damages you.

It is possible to build a long term relationship with someone who is suffering from NPD, but, it will take a huge amount of patience and dedication as well as a commitment from the sufferer to seek professional assistance and slowly overcome their issues. For you to stand by someone with this condition and attempt to build a solid relationship, you must have a good support network in place; you will need someone to turn to and this person may also need to be the one who gives you the strength to walk away if there is nothing more you can do.

Research has shown that people with NPD can improve over time via the use of appropriate stimulation, achieving realistic goals and even building on existing relationships. This will enable anyone to handle criticism and manage disappointment in their life; this is two of the key skills that anyone with narcissistic personality disorder needs to develop. They may never be able to empathize with others but they will gain an understanding of how their actions can hurt others and can learn to adjust their behavior and responses accordingly.

To ensure your relationship survives and your partner develops more normal responses to situations it is essential to educate them at every opportunity you get. As well as locating reading material concerning the disorder you will need to prepare examples of how each attribute manifests itself in their behavior and the effect it has on the people around them. The response may be typically aggressive, but after several attempts even the staunchest of self-believers will start to see the truth in your information; they then need to be willing to change.

Education is also an important part of the family and loved ones accepting the sufferer as who they are. It can and will help them to become better at healthy interaction with other people.

Conclusion

One major reason why narcissists continue to overpower you is because you allow them to by not establishing healthy boundaries in your relationships.

Boundaries are crucial to success because they help the people involved in a relationship understand the parameters of the bond and what they must and must not do.

For instance, if you do not ever talk to your friend about how you do not appreciate the fact that he/she lies to his/her mother about spending time with you whereas he/she is actually hanging out with his/her drug addict friends, he/she is likely to continue with that and throw more dirt on you.

Similarly, if you don't tell your narcissistic spouse that his/ her dominating behavior annoys you and that he/ she must sort out their act if he/ she want to continue living with you peacefully, he/ she will only continue to do the same.

Chances are that your spouse may still behave the same way even if you communicate your concerns with them, but if you keep acting decisively, you will be able to modify their behavior soon.

Here is what you need to do to become assertive with the narcissists in your life and change their irrational behavior.

Understand What You Want and Set Boundaries Accordingly

First and most importantly, spend some time reflecting on what you expect from your relationship with the narcissist. Wrap your head around one thing: he/ she is incapable of loving you like you hope for, and while there is hope for them to improve, do not expect them to transform into a completely optimistic, supportive and loving individual because their thought process has now become quite distorted.

So while thinking of the expectations you have about them and how you would like for them to behave with you, think as rationally as possible.

List down the things you want that person to keep in mind when interacting with you and set boundaries accordingly. If you want your partner to stop playing the blame game, communicate that concern with him/her. If you want your sibling to stop yelling at you every time you don't pay follow his/her demands, inform him/her of that firmly.

Make Sure the Boundaries are respected and Reach a Compromise with them

When you do set certain boundaries with your narcissist partner or friend, make sure he/ she observes them. Keep a check on his/ her behavior and if you observe him/ her breaching the limits, have a firm talk with him/ her one last time. Even if you do not wish to leave him/ her, tell him/ her that you may have to do that if they push you to that and in that case, separate from him/ her for a few days if the need arises.

Also, inform the narcissist that you are only living with them or carrying on with the relationship you have with him/ her if they choose to compromise. Talk to them about how suffocated you feel and how you are now in the position to live independently, but since you have spent quite a long time with them and respect that, you wish to stay on good terms with them if they respect you back. Be very firm when you say that and try not to cry or show your emotions because that again can weaken you and put them in the power position.

Play with their Feelings like They Do with Yours

Always remember that a narcissist in any relationship views the other person as his/ her competitor. There is no concept of having the middle way in a relationship or giving love, as they expect to receive because they only expect to get what they want irrespective of their behavior with the other person.

In any relationship, they can only see in terms of the top dog who is like the alpha dog, giving directions to others and an underdog, one who pays heed to the top dog and tries to act more like him. A narcissist only wishes to be perceived as the top dog, so when you try to turn things around, he/ she is likely to become hyper-alert and look for ways to return to the alpha position.

They have quite an inflated ego which they do not want to lose at any cost. So when you try to act assertively with them, they will play even harder to hurt you and will always act as if they are competing with you. So if you try to hold your partner's hand, he/she may jerk yours to hurt your feelings. If you ask your friend to go out for drinks with you, he/she may refuse your offer to because you pain.

If you wish to outsmart a narcissist, you need to go as low as possible to match their emotional frequency. You can do two things. First, you can give him/ her regular assurance that you are not competing with them or trying to prove that you are better than him/ her. This should be in case that narcissist is the vulnerable type. If he/ she belong to the grandiose category, you too need to hurt him/ her a little. Stop making attempts to appease him/ her when he/ she is upset; do not go out of the way to make him/ her feel comfortable; and stop checking up on him/ her to ensure they are doing okay.

Just look after yourself and do not act as his/ her guardian or care taker at all. When you stop tending to his/ her petty needs and acting like his/ her care provider, he/ she will soon realize that you have changed. He/ she will then try to hurt you or apologize to you. In both cases, inform him/ her of how unacceptable his/ her behavior is and that you will not take any of that nonsense again. Remember to be firm at all costs and you will only break him/ her further.

Use the Word 'NO' when Needed

Throughout our lives, we have been told that 'sorry', 'please' and 'thank you' are the 3 magic words you need to use to win people's hearts. While this is true, these words often do not work with narcissists. In fact, they only give them too much reassurance which makes them get on your nerves.

To effectively and tactfully handle a narcissist, you need to create a new vocabulary of magic words for him/ her and the first word in the list is 'no.' Narcissists yearn to hear 'yes' to everything they demand from others. If they want you to stand on one leg the entire day, they expect you to oblige. They want you to take them on expensive trips and they won't hear 'no' for an answer. Often, the problem in narcissistic relationships is that due to the fear of upsetting a narcissist, you are likely to say 'yes' to all his/ her demands. While you hope for your sacrifices to make him/ her nicer person, he/ she won't ever change.

Instead of agreeing to everything he/ she wants, start saying 'no' more often. If a narcissist comes up with an unacceptable demand, firmly reject it. Yes, it will upset him/ her and may even make him/ her act irrationally, but you need to stick to the 'no' in any case. Just do it a few times, distance yourself from them and do not budge from your stance in any case, and within a couple of weeks, they will get used to hearing no from you. While they may stay grumpy, so be it because you need some peace as well.

Challenge them

Narcissists lie in different and strange ways. Sometimes, they exaggerate things to come off as a superior individual, and on other occasions, they can fabricate the biggest of lies to bring you down, or even make fantasies involving them. This can be very annoying and if you keep up with this behavior, you will only play a role in inflating their ego.

You need to challenge them by asking them for a proof every time they make a claim that seems false. Demand evidence that proves their claim and clearly show that you doubt their story. When they feel challenged, they are likely to budge from their stance, or stop making stories the next time.

Tell Them They Don't Scare You

A good way to neutralize someone with a narcissistic personality is to inform them of how they do not scare you. Such people are insecure and wish to turn on the insecurities of others too. They observe the insecurities and weaknesses of others to exploit them when the need arises.

If any narcissist you would like to change does that to you, fend him/ her off by telling him/ her of how his/ her tactics do not scare you. If he/ she become furious let he / she explode because that is clearly not your problem. Do not comfort him/ her at that point because again, that is not your concern.

Don't Talk to Them until Necessary

Do not talk to your narcissistic friends or loved ones unless absolutely necessary. When you try to neutralize their effect, they will want to get back to you.

So your partner told you she is upset and needs you, but you know she only wants to try her hand at controlling you again so you tell her you are busy. This is likely to challenge something which will compel her to try to talk to you time and again. When that happens, avoid talking to her completely.

You need to prove to the other person that you are strong enough to survive on your own, and can do really well in life even when they are not around. Since narcissists are lonely and do not have many people to seek support from, when they see you drifting apart, they are likely to improve on their act.

If you do see the narcissists in your life improving after a few months, show them compassion and love, but always in moderation because too much comfort can again put them in the power position. Soon, the two of you will establish a workable relationship that will neither burden you nor him/ her. However, if he/ she becomes abusive to the extent that he/ she resorts to physical, sexual and extreme psychological abuse to manipulate you, it is best to think things through and bring in a lawyer and legal authorities to save yourself from any irreparable harm. While you may not want to leave him/ her, there may come a time when you have to, and in that case, it is best to save yourself now than feel sorry later.

Lightning Source UK Ltd.
Milton Keynes UK
UKHW021218171220
375314UK00003B/228